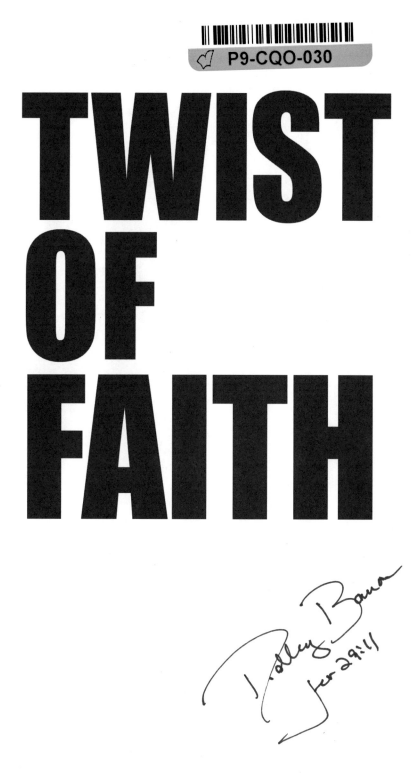

TWIST OF FAITH

ONE TRAGEDY SHATTERED HIS WORLD

TWIST OF FAITH

ONE CHOICE FREED HIM TO HEAL

RIDLEY BARRON

Ridley Barron Ministries
hope - healing - forgiveness

Dedicated to the memory of loved ones lost and the joy of new loves found. To God be all the glory for showing us the Hope we all can have.

PROLOGUE

Good Friday, April 9, 2004, broke brilliantly on Hilton Head Island, South Carolina. Warmth and sunshine slowly awakened the countryside, providing a contrast to the cooler, cloudy days that had preceded it. It was a nice reminder that spring had arrived.

Even though my wife and kids and I were in the final hours of what had been an incredible spring break trip, our day started like so many others: Josh, our youngest, was the first to stir, followed closely by his sister, Abby, and older brother, Harrison. Other than the little hotel room the five of us were packed into, and the need to load luggage and toys into our van for the journey home, there was nothing unusual about the day.

Home was Douglas, Georgia, a small town of about 20,000 people in the southeast part of the state. This was where we had moved to plant a church in August of 2000. It was where my wife, Sarah Ellen, and the kids and I had lived for the past four years. Although the trip was normally about four hours, Sarah Ellen and I had decided to take our time in making our way home. It wasn't often that we were able to get away like this. We had enjoyed the much-needed break from the demands of our ministry responsibilities and did not want to rush back into our daily schedules too quickly.

The first stop on the return trip was a leisurely breakfast at a restaurant on the island. Our kids paused to play with some ducks in the parking lot there before all five of us loaded back into our seats. The van's back end was packed with golf clubs, suitcases, a stroller, and several bags of newly purchased school clothes. I took my normal place in the driver's seat, with Sarah Ellen in the passenger seat next to me. Behind us was a split bench seat that held all three kids. Abby, age six at the time, sat immediately behind Sarah Ellen. She was our only girl and, of course, had Daddy wrapped around her finger. Her blond hair was radiant in the sunlight, and the back seat was filled with her laughter as she did her best to stay one step ahead of her two brothers.

Next to her, in the middle of the seat, was my oldest son, Harrison. At age nine, he was the mirror image of me in both his looks and his temperament. Much of our free time together was spent tossing a ball or wrestling around on our den floor. I also enjoyed watching him play sports and was pleased to be coaching his Little League baseball team, which was midway through its season.

Harrison had been a "surprise," conceived before Sarah Ellen and I had celebrated our third wedding anniversary. We called him our miracle baby too, because despite having to fight his way through some first-trimester complications that Sarah had with the pregnancy, he'd been born a completely healthy and very vibrant little boy.

Finally, immediately behind the driver's seat was the newest addition to the Barron family, Joshua. Josh was approaching eighteen months old and was a constant joy. Many people had told us that parenting would get easier with our third child because by then, we would better understand what we were doing and what was required. I chose to believe that Josh just made it easy. His personality was so alive for someone so young. Both of his older siblings were absolutely crazy about him and would often fight over who would take care of him.

Just the night before, on Thursday, the entire family had enjoyed some time in the hotel swimming pool. We had used the opportunity to begin introducing Josh to the water and teaching him how to swim. To close out the evening, he and I had snuggled in our bed and watched the Braves game as he snacked on potato chips. It was an amazing evening.

As we traveled home, we made several other stops, including a short shopping trip—much to Harrison's chagrin. School would be back in session on Monday, and Sarah Ellen wanted to get a few more clothes for our rapidly growing kids. We enjoyed a late lunch and let the kids burn off a little energy on a playground while Sarah Ellen and I talked. Afterwards, we took a side trip into Savannah to pick up a few things for our church at a local Christian bookstore.

With Easter Sunday just ahead, there were some loose ends to wrap up in preparation for such a big weekend in the life of our young church. We had planted GracePointe Church four years before in Douglas. We loved those people very deeply, and they were very much a part of our lives. Our last stop was about forty-five minutes from our house. Although the kids had a DVD to entertain them, they were beginning to get a little antsy. The older two needed to use the restroom, and Sarah and I were both ready to stretch our legs a bit, so we stopped at a convenience store in Hazlehurst, Georgia, to let everyone have a break.

As we returned to the van, I asked Sarah Ellen if she would mind driving the rest of the way to our house. I wanted to finalize my thoughts before delivering my Sunday morning message, but I had another motive as well. Just the day before, we had received the call to come back to Middle Tennessee. At the invitation of our former church in Nashville, we would be returning in a few months to suburban Franklin—a place we had lived for six years while serving a church there—to begin our second church plant. I was laying out plans for our new church and thought this last leg of the trip would be a great time to do some goal setting without interruption. Sarah Ellen agreed, so we secured our kids in their places and she and I swapped seats.

The rest of our trip home would be on rural roads through the beautiful South Georgia countryside.

1

Farms, ponds, country houses, and a few fluffy clouds dotted the scenery over the next several miles as we drove back to our home in Douglas, Georgia, on that Good Friday. Before too long, Sarah turned on her blinker and maneuvered onto a road that I was unfamiliar with. Looking up from my reading, I asked where we were going.

"Taking a shortcut," she replied. "It will save us about fifteen minutes."

Sarah Ellen had been selling custom jewelry for a couple of years, and this involved home shows and visits to local events. In the process, she had learned many of the backroads and shortcuts around Coffee County. She was letting me in on one of her new secrets.

I turned back to the book I was reading and my final preparations for the Easter message I would deliver on Sunday. Suddenly Sarah Ellen shouted, "Oh my word!" Then . . . darkness.

How long I was out, I'm not sure. But the sound of Harrison's voice over my left shoulder aroused me from unconsciousness. He was half crying, half shouting at me, "Daddy! Daddy! What's happening? Are we okay? What's wrong with Mommy?"

I awoke to a very dreamlike state. I couldn't decide if I had fallen asleep and missed part of the trip, or if something completely different was going on. I just knew that my head was very clouded.

But when I heard Harrison's alarming question of "What's wrong with Mommy?" I got my first glance at the driver's seat. My wife's seat was laid back, her head against the headrest and her breathing very labored. Instinctively, I tried to reach over to her, but I couldn't move—my legs were pinned in by the crumpled dash. I also felt severe pain in my left shoulder, and though my body was feeling very stiff and achy—calling to mind the first few days of football camp where every muscle in my body would ache from the hours of impact—everything else seemed to be in working order. (I would later learn that my left humerus was broken just below the shoulder joint, and my right wrist had been broken in the accident as well.)

I could not undo my seat belt, so I strained to touch Sarah Ellen. It was to no avail; I was stuck.

I was also very disoriented. The only thing that was clear was that something horrible had happened. Our van was settled backwards into a ditch about sixty yards from the intersection through which we had just passed. To my left, tall Georgia pines guarded the far side of the two-lane road.

The front windshield was shattered, and the dashboard was crushed. The window on Sarah's side of the van had broken out completely, and her neck was at a weird angle.

The next thing I knew, a man I had never seen before was peering through the driver's side window and trying to rouse my wife: "Ma'am! Ma'am! Are you okay? Can you talk to me?" The tone of his voice and the dire look on his face were unsettling.

Sarah was not answering.

When she tried to turn her head in my direction, I grew more alarmed and screamed, "Sarah! Sarah! Wake up, baby. It's going to be okay." Then I begged her: "Sarah! Sarah! Talk to me."

Still nothing.

In the distance I could hear approaching sirens. The stranger had worked his way around the front of our van and was now leaning through my busted window. "Sir, are you okay? Is there anything I can do for you?"

I ignored his question, my every thought focused on Sarah. She slowly rolled her head back to the center of the headrest, and a huge breath escaped her lips, almost as if she was sighing with pain. The man repeated his question more adamantly, "Sir, are you okay?"

"I think so," I snapped. "Would you please just take care of my wife?"

"Sir, I don't think there is anything we can do for her."

His words caught me by surprise and took my breath. I

began to cry. The tears burned as they rolled down my face. Cuts that had been opened up by flying glass in the accident were now filling with salt. I did the only thing I could think to do: I closed my eyes and began to talk with God. Years of Sunday School answers and Bible verses escaped me now. All I could manage were a few desperate sentences: "God, You won't let her die. You can't. It's not fair . . . I can't be alone; I won't make it by myself."

To this day, I will not forget the sense of peace that entered the car at that moment. Nothing about the situation had changed; I simply felt more in control of my thoughts and actions. I believe God wanted to remind me that I still had three kids to take care of.

I took one last glance at Sarah, still praying that she would suddenly turn and face me again with those beautiful blue eyes of hers. Nothing.

Harrison was screaming more loudly now, having picked up on the conversation in the front seat. "Daddy, what's going on with Mommy? Why isn't she talking?"

"It's okay, buddy." *Was I trying to convince him or myself?* "Everything's okay. Mommy is just a little hurt."

Wrestling with my seat belt, I twisted as best I could to try and calm him. My legs and arms were pinned so tightly that I could not see Abby at all. "It's okay, buddy," I reassured him. "Everything's going to be all right. How's Abby?"

"I don't know, Daddy. She's not moving or talking."

"Abby. Abby! It's Daddy . . . Can you hear me? . . . Are you okay?"

By this point, I was afraid that my worst fears were multiplying. But then I heard in a very hushed tone from the back seat, "I'm okay, Daddy. I'm alright." I could tell by her voice that she was in shock, unsure of what had happened, afraid of what she didn't know.

Wrestling even more with my seat belt, I twisted my head around as far as I could, wanting to lay eyes on my kids. For the first time, I was able to free myself enough to see in the seat behind Sarah's. It was empty; Josh and his car seat were no longer in the van with us.

Panic filled me. I peered as far back into the van as I could to be sure that Josh hadn't been tossed to the rear of the vehicle. He wasn't there either.

I noticed that many of the windows had been broken out in the crash. Putting two and two together, I concluded that Josh must have been thrown from the vehicle when the van rolled over. Instantly, I turned to the stranger and screamed at him, "Sir, you've got to find my son! There is a third child and he's missing! Go find him! He must have been thrown from the van!" With those words, the man disappeared to start the search.

Others who had arrived on the scene joined him, and together they frantically scoured the side of the road.

That's when time began to crawl for me. I prayed harder. "God, this can't be happening. It's got to be a dream. Help me. I am so scared right now. Will You take care of my wife? Please, let her be okay. She's got to be okay."

I was crying, begging, and negotiating all at the same time. "God, my kids don't deserve this. Neither does Sarah. Take me! The kids would be okay with her. They need their mom. Please, God. Please." I must have repeated the word *please* a hundred times. It was the one word that kept surfacing in my mind.

Over the course of those few desperate minutes in the van—amid all the chaos—something unexpected happened in my heart. First, God and I began a conversation that would go on for the next several months with increasing intensity. Second, and most importantly, God's presence became more real for me. I sensed him reminding me, "Ridley, you are not going to be alone. Haven't I always promised that? Now, just trust me. *We* will get through this . . . I promise."

The moment was broken by the voice of one of the firemen working to free my legs. "Sir, we've found your other son. He's going to be okay. They are getting him ready for transport in an ambulance now. Now, let's see what we can do about getting the rest of your family out of here."

One trip was over—one of the best vacations our family had ever had together. Another was just beginning—a much longer, more difficult one than I could ever have imagined. My family and I were about to embark on a journey like nothing we'd ever experienced.

2

There was twenty to thirty feet of grass between the road's edge and the tall, slender pines that stood along the far edges of the ditch where our van ended up after the collision. I was told later that it was under those pines that the stranger who'd been the first on the scene found Josh, unconscious and face down, still strapped in his car seat. Using his knowledge of infant CPR, this gentleman was able to revive Josh before the paramedics arrived.

While Josh was found in a matter of minutes, it seemed like forever before the firefighters had extricated the rest of us from the van. A boogie board from the back of our van was placed along the edge of the road, and emergency personnel seated Harrison and Abby there as they tended to them. While I waited to be removed from the van, I allowed myself to slump back into my seat and close my eyes. I was totally unable to control anything around me. Yet the mass of people at the scene gave me a strange sense of comfort.

Once free of the wreckage, I was placed immediately on a backboard and immobilized with a neck brace. All I could see as I was being escorted to the ambulance was the brilliant blue sky. I remember thinking what a contrast that serene sky was to the desperate chaos all around me. The EMTs placed Abby and Harrison into an ambulance with the "bad guys," as Abby would later describe them—the three young men who had run their stop sign at fifty to sixty miles an hour, striking the front left side of our van and sending us on our deadly roll down the side of the highway.

As I was being slid into the ambulance, I could hear more frantic activity all around me. I had only been strapped into place for a few minutes when the doors opened and one of the paramedics appeared at my side. "Mr. Barron. Your son . . . Josh is his name?"

"Yes," I mumbled through the restraints around my head.

"Some people found Josh over in the trees. He is being placed in the vehicle with you. He is doing okay, but he has a pretty bad head injury and is in a lot of pain. I need you to try to talk to him—let him know you are here. See if you can't calm him a little with your voice."

Through my tears, I began to speak gently, "Josh. It's Daddy . . ." His only response was a moaning noise, which indicated to me that he was in a lot of pain. It was a sound that he repeatedly made on the fifteen-minute trip to the hospital.

The ambulance sirens soon drowned out all other noises. I was so anxious to get to the hospital and find out what was happening to my family that I spent the entire ride trying to imagine where we were based on the turns the vehicle was taking. Sometime during the trip to the hospital, though, I mustered up the courage to ask one of the EMTs, "My wife . . . Is she okay? Did she make it?"

He responded with silence. I couldn't decide if this meant he was too busy to hear me or too afraid to tell me what was going on. Afraid and uncertain, I soaked the padding of my neck brace with my tears.

The sirens quieted once we pulled up to the hospital entrance. As I was rolled back to the emergency room, I could see hundreds of people in the parking lot and waiting room. As soon as I was secured in one of the curtained areas, it seemed like a dozen people swarmed to my side. In a few minutes, a nurse came and asked if there was anyone I would like to contact. I told her yes. She disappeared momentarily and returned to my side with a cordless phone, dialing the numbers I gave her. Then she patiently held the phone to my ear as I relayed the news of what had happened to each of my sisters.

My younger sister was on the way back to Douglas from spring break with her own family; my oldest sister lived in Columbus, Georgia, with her family—three hours away. I decided to leave it to one of them to break the news to my mom. She was still in mourning after losing Dad just two months earlier. My dad had passed away from complications due to diabetes and congestive heart problems after a ten-year battle. They had been married for more than forty-five years.

I would also leave it to them to begin the task of calling Sarah's family.

Just as I completed the phone calls, Dr. Stephanie Barber came to my bedside. Stephanie was our pediatrician and a family friend who also attended our church. Sarah and Stephanie had sat in Bible studies and enjoyed lunches together over the past several months as their friendship grew. She was literally the first familiar face I saw after the accident.

With great tenderness and compassion, our friend placed herself at my bedside and began to work to calm me. Stephanie had kids of her own—a fact that I believe helped guide her response in that moment.

"What can I do for you, Ridley? What do you need?" she asked.

"Stephanie, where are the kids? What's going on with my family? No one is telling me anything. What about the kids? Are they okay?"

She began to recount what she knew. "Abby is doing fine. She had some seat belt bruising, but she's okay. They are going to send her home tonight with your sister's family. Harrison has some head injuries. I feel confident he is fine, but we want to run some tests and keep him overnight for observation. He's very restless right now, which is a good sign. They are going to begin those tests in just a few minutes."

She hesitated, then continued, "Josh had a really bad head injury. I think he will be okay as well, but I want to be sure. While I think we could take care of his needs here, I want your permission to send him over to the hospital in Savannah, where they can give him better care. It's a precautionary measure but, if it were me, I'd probably want that to happen. Are you okay with that?" I quickly agreed, knowing Stephanie had my kids' best interest at heart.

Then came this giant silence. Stephanie knew what had yet to be asked; I knew what I was desperate to know. Finally, fighting back more tears, I asked, "What about Sarah? What's going on with her?" My throat was closing up and the neck collar made it harder to get the words out even as I spoke them. But I also instinctively knew the answer. Before Stephanie told me, I knew. I knew because the stranger's expression had told me. I knew because the EMT's silence had seemed so ominous. I knew because a husband just knows these things when he has lost his best friend.

Stephanie's eyes filled with tears as she shared the news that no man ever wants to hear about the woman he loves.

As Stephanie and I continued to talk, my children were being cared for in different parts of the ER. In a room not far from where I lay, another friend of ours, Janie—who was also Abby's Sunday school teacher—was entertaining Abby by playing games on a dry-erase board. Though Janie was doing her best to keep my daughter distracted, before long, Abby asked the question that we all were asking: "Is Mommy okay?"

Janie sent for my sister Tonda, who, along with her

family, had just arrived at the hospital. Tonda came into the room, pulled her niece into her lap, and did the only thing she knew to do: she prayed with Abby for her mom. Yes, she had been informed that Sarah was dead. But she also knew that this is what Sarah would have done for Abby in such a moment if the situation had been reversed.

Harrison, meanwhile, was undergoing the tests to determine his condition . . . but not willingly. He was agitated, even combative. The doctors and nurses tried to keep him still long enough to do X-rays. Tonda made her way to Harrison's side and tried her best to console him, but he was not to be comforted.

While she was with Harrison, I was joined by one of my best buddies, Rusty Fender. He, too, was a church member. He was also a local car dealer—the very one I had bought the van from. He would later tell me his heart was crushed when he heard the news. I remember him saying, "Ridley, I swear that was the safest vehicle I had, or I wouldn't have put your family in it."

That went without saying. I knew how Rusty felt about my family—our boys were teammates, and our wives were dear friends. Yet even the safest vehicle couldn't guarantee protection when two vehicles collide at fifty miles an hour or more.

Next thing I knew, the curtain parted and Tonda came in to check on me. Seeing her there made my emotions erupt. I was feeling anger and sadness all at once. I wanted to scream, to cry, to let out all that was boiling up inside. Most of all, I wanted to get rid of that neck brace and get off of that gurney so I could see my family.

"I'm going to be sick. I think I'm gonna throw up," I mumbled as I tugged at the brace.

"Stop, Ridley. You can't do that," she said. "They haven't gotten your tests back yet; you could hurt yourself." She sounded like a sister. And for now, that was quite all right with me.

Tonda stayed for just a little while before slipping back out through the curtain to go check on the kids again. I think she was afraid I would ask her about Sarah. I'm not sure she realized I already knew.

Hours passed. I would later find out that members of my church and the community had crowded the hospital to the point that people were being sent away. As my family arrived at my bedside, I couldn't help but think about how each of us—especially my mom—was still mourning my dad's death in our own way. Now, that mourning had been cut short by a new focus for our sorrow.

My emotions were very raw. And now that my entire family was gathered at my side, I felt I could allow my mind to wander.

I caught myself thinking backward and forward at the same time. I flashed back over the thirteen years that Sarah and I had together. I remembered the first time I ever noticed her (singing in the choir at our church in Macon,

Georgia). I remembered the first time I kissed her (as we stood in the doorway at her parents' house) and the first time I ever told her I loved her (while we sat in the parking lot of a school where we had stopped to talk and pray). I thought about our wedding on that warm July day just a year later. We'd enjoyed precious memories together in our 600-square foot apartment in Fort Worth, Texas, while I was attending seminary.

Then one haunting memory popped into my head as I lay there: the day we drove down to Douglas to move into our new house and start the church. She had cried a good part of the trip, partially out of fear of the unknown that awaited, and partially out of love for all the things we were leaving behind. Suddenly an awful thought crossed my mind: *Had I been wrong to bring Sarah to Douglas? Did she resent me for taking her out of Franklin, a town and a church we deeply loved?* I wept as this singular thought washed over me—I would never know the answer to these questions because there would never be another memory between the two of us. Not one.

I also wondered what the future would look like without her. Sarah and I had talked a great deal about the "what ifs" should one of us die. The loss of her eleven-year-old niece, Taylor, in November the year before, and my dad's passing in February, had given us plenty of reason to have those conversations. Taylor—the daughter of Sarah's brother, Clay—had died due to a perforated appendix. It was a tragic, unexpected death that ripped at our hearts. She was so precious, so full of life. My dad had passed away three months later. Both of those events had caused Sarah and me to spend several long car rides from Birmingham, Alabama (where Clay and his family lived), and Columbus, Georgia (where my father is buried), talking about the future.

The ironic thing is that I always believed I was preparing my wife for my eventual death. Those conversations were meant to get Sarah ready for the day she'd have to pick up the pieces and go on without me. Little did I know that God was stirring *my* heart and making it ready for what was about to happen in my life.

In spite of those conversations, though, I had no idea how I would raise our kids without their mom. Or what my life would look like without my best friend by my side. Or how our kids would handle the news when I finally broke it to them. These were just the beginning of the questions that were on my mind.

Soon, a helicopter arrived to transport Josh to Savannah. There, he would be under the care of specialists who could monitor his situation. As the day wore on, Abby was taken to my sister's house to hang out with her cousins and their Aunt Kema. Harrison was admitted to a private room in the ICU, down the hallway from my room. My sister Harriet promised to keep a watchful eye on him through the night while her husband, Richard, volunteered to stay with me.

It would be a restless night despite the medications.

3

I'm not sure what woke me up on Saturday morning. Maybe it was the clinking of equipment or the beep of monitors by my bed. I blinked my eyes and shut them just as quickly. Was it all a dream . . . a really bad one? The past eighteen hours were so foggy. Maybe it had been just one horrible nightmare.

I opened my eyes to see my mother, my oldest sister, and both of my brothers-in-law standing at the foot of my hospital bed. My fears had been realized. The nightmare was real.

My sister Harriet moved from the end of the bed to be by my side. "How are you feeling, Ridley?"

"Like I've been in a car wreck," I joked, trying to laugh without hurting. "Where are the kids? What's going on?"

A nurse who was standing in the doorway shifted her weight as Harriet updated me. "Abby is at Tonda and Keith's house with the boys. Harrison is in another room. He woke up earlier this morning and has eaten some breakfast. He's waiting to see you. Would you like for me to bring him in?"

It was about 5 a.m. Evidently we'd both had a restless night.

I nodded. This would not be an easy conversation.

Within a few minutes, Harriet wheeled Harrison into my room in a wheelchair. This was my first indication of his troubled heart. Any other time, my nine-year-old would have had a big grin on his face at the prospect of tooling around in a wheelchair. Yet there was no smile this time; only a worried look. I started as casually as possible.

"Hey, buddy. How are you feeling this morning?"

Harrison wasted no time. "Daddy, what happened to Mom? Is Mom dead?"

"Yeah, Harrison, Mommy's gone. She died in the wreck."

The fierceness with which he rubbed his forehead made his red face even redder. The tears were pouring from his eyes as he fought to speak. "What are we going to do for a mom?"

Initially, I was torn up by this question. How could he be asking such a thing less than twenty-four hours after his mom had died? *Replace her.* That was not the first thing on my mind. Getting out of the bed and going home to find out what pieces were left of our family was a bigger priority to me.

Since that day, though, God has shown me the beauty behind that question. Harrison was a child, thinking as only children can. All he had ever known was Sarah and me together. Having his mom and dad in their normal places meant security and stability for him. So, in the aftermath of this whirlwind that had shaken his world, Harrison was doing the same thing I was: trying to figure out how to get back to "normal" and learn what it would take to be back in that place of security.

I said the only thing I knew to say at that point: "We'll just have to see, buddy. I know you miss your mommy. We all do. But what happens next is up to God."

I don't even know that I believed those words myself as they came out of my mouth. But they were all I had.

I asked the nurse to let Harrison crawl up into the bed with me. He and I lay there together, sobbing and holding each other. It would not be the last time we shared that kind of moment together.

Later that morning, I would have to repeat the conversation yet again, with similar reaction. My mother brought Abby to the hospital so I could break the news to her. Then, Harrison and I were released to go home . . . whatever home might be for us now.

Once my brother-in-law, Richard, eased his Tahoe into the driveway that Saturday, I slid from the front seat and slowly moved toward the front door of our house while the rest of the family surrounded the vehicle to escort Abby and Harrison indoors. Every inch of my body ached from the impact the day before—my back, my head, my legs. But while I had broken my left arm and right wrist, nothing hurt worse than my heart.

There were cars in the driveway and street in front of the house—indicators of the many people who had gathered inside. Yet it was so strange, knowing that my beautiful wife would not be there waiting, nor would her personality be warming our home ever again. Walking up the sidewalk to our front door, I felt like I was entering someone else's house—like I was just a guest in this place we'd called home. Sarah and I had been so close for the twelve years of our marriage that the idea of waking up without her and living on without her made my mind whirl.

I stepped gingerly into the family room and was greeted by family members and friends who had gathered to make sure we were okay. Before long, we adults found ourselves around the kitchen table: Mrs. Trimble (Sarah's mom), Tricia and Neil (her sister and brother-in-law), and my family. Tonda was the only one missing. After making sure that we were all okay the night before, she had rushed to Savannah to be at Josh's bedside so that when he awoke, a familiar face would be there to greet him.

The group of us talked about many things before our conversation turned to the funeral arrangements. Everyone was shocked to find that I already knew what I wanted for Sarah.

It was agreed that we would do a memorial service at our church in Douglas on Monday morning. Then, we would have her body transported to Tennessee (where the kids and I would be relocating) for a funeral service at our former church in Nashville on Friday. Forest Hills Church had been such a huge part of our lives that we knew we wanted to celebrate Sarah's life with those people. Having her buried in nearby Franklin was a no-brainer as well.

Not long after we wrapped up the conversation, the doorbell rang. It was Dr. Kevin Trapnell—my personal physician, friend, and one of the leaders in our church. He was coming by to check on me and to bring me medication to help me sleep. The way people loved on us and cared for us during that time was truly humbling.

Kevin had also come to ask who should be contacted about filling in for me the next morning at church. *Dang*, I thought to myself, *it's Easter.*

"No one," I said, as shocked by my reply as anyone.

"Are you sure?" he asked. The people sitting around us in the den repeated the question, as if to verify that I had heard him correctly.

"Yes. I'm sure. If I can't preach about life and death and eternity after what has happened to my family this week, who can?" And with that, it was decided that I would stand before the people of GracePointe on Easter Sunday morning—bruises, cuts, sling, and all.

4

Ahost of people stood outside the front door to our church that Easter Sunday morning. As a church plant with no elegant house of worship to call our own, we had begun in an abandoned bar at the edge of town. Our people had cleaned up the property, ripped out the carpet, and repainted the entire building. As God blessed us and we continued to grow, we turned the bar into space for our youth and kids, and secured use of a clothing store just across the parking lot. It was there that we would have our memorial service on Monday. But for now it was Easter, and a crowd was gathering for the church service.

Many were there out of curiosity that day. Douglas is a small town, and news of the accident had spread quickly over the weekend. Plenty of people came for no other reason than to see what I would say and how I would act. Others were there to show their support. Friends from all over the state came to encourage and stand by our family in those desperate days. It was good to see them; their presence would be critical to our journey—even our survival— over the next few years.

The Easter service was packed with emotion. For me, there were intense moments—brought on by some song or comment—where I could barely endure Sarah's absence. When the time came for me to deliver my message, I felt unsure about how I would be able to get through it. What happened in those next few minutes is hard to describe. Stepping to the top level of the tiered stage, I turned to face some of the most precious people I knew—and a sea of faces that I didn't. The crowd was double what our normal attendance would have been on an Easter Sunday, with a hundred or more new visitors. I told them:

> I'm here today because of the power that was given to us that first Easter. I'm here because it's what Sarah would expect and what she would desire. I have ultimate confidence that she is alive and well and in a place that you and I both want to be someday.
>
> I want to talk to you about all the evidence that exists to prove that Jesus did indeed die that Friday afternoon 2,000 years ago. But there is equal evidence —overwhelming evidence—to prove that Jesus was raised from the dead by the power of His Father. And that same power gives us hope of a future resurrection and a future with Him in heaven.

I got emotional and was even overcome by my grief more than once. But I believe that God enabled me to deliver a message on death and life and Jesus' resurrection that I could not have given without His intervention.

I closed the sermon that day by quoting the powerful words of one of Sarah's favorite worship songs.

Sing to the King who is coming to reign
Glory to Jesus, the Lamb that was slain
Life and salvation His empire shall bring
And joy to the nations, when Jesus is King

Come, let us sing a song
A song declaring we belong
To Jesus
He is all we need
Lift up a heart of praise
Sing now with voices raised
To Jesus
Sing to the King

For His returning we watch and we pray
We will be ready the dawn of that day
We'll join in singing with all the redeemed
'Cause Satan is vanquished and Jesus is King![1]

When I finished, one young lady who Sarah had mentored walked up to the front of the church and, with tears in her eyes, shared that Sarah's life had been an example to her for many months. Though Sarah had so desperately prayed

---

for her, it was fear that had kept this woman from surrendering her life to Christ. But Sarah's death had shown her there was something more worth living for. So she prayed to give her life to Christ and follow Him in the closing moments of that Easter service.

I thought to myself, *Even in death, Sarah's life is touching others.* Then, there was this immediate impression that God was saying to me, "This is just the beginning, Ridley. Trust Me. You will see the good that can come, even in the midst of your darkest moments. I am big enough."

5

People began to arrive at the house early on Monday morning for Sarah's memorial service in Douglas. My mom's family had come from southwest Georgia. Sarah's family came from Macon and Atlanta. Probably a dozen of our friends from Nashville were there, along with numerous friends from Alabama and North Carolina.

Before we left the house that morning, my entire family gathered in our den—more than sixty of us. I love my family. They have been such a huge part of who I am and what God has taught me throughout life. I took this time to thank every single one of them for coming and standing with the kids and me. I knew they were busy; I knew their lives were as hectic as mine. Yet their willingness to sacrifice and come and lock arms with us as we walked through this difficulty was a tremendous blessing. I wanted them to know that before we began the day.

My cousin Bruce prayed a prayer as we held hands: "God, thank You for family. It's family that walks with us in the darkest of moments. It's family that keeps us clinging to You when it would seem easier to let go . . ."

Once the "amen" had been said and lots of hugs were exchanged, we were off to GracePointe Church for the memorial service.

When we arrived at the church in the car provided by the funeral home, Abby and Harrison eased themselves out of the back seat, with me just behind them. What we were met with that day, I can only describe as unbelievable. The crowd that had attended our church's worship service the day before paled in comparison to the mass of people who were there for the memorial. The entire parking area for the strip mall was filled, and the funeral home staff was shuttling people from a nearby church's parking lot. The worship room chairs were filled, and people lined the walls.

I was completely humbled by the outpouring of love that day. Some of our closest friends from Middle Tennessee made the trip down. There were friends from Macon, where Sarah had grown up, and friends from Columbus, where I had spent most of my days as a teen.

Of course, the town of Douglas was there in full support too. Some of these friends got up and shared stories and memories of Sarah. Others spoke of Sarah's impact on their lives. Tonda and Keith, who served as worship leaders for our church, stood before all of us that morning and—with the help of their fellow worship team members—led us in a time of praise to God.

The service was just as Sarah and I had discussed. Yes, there were tears and sadness, but mostly we celebrated Sarah and her life. We celebrated what she brought to others and how she had influenced every single one of us in her own special way.

Both of my children sat closer than usual that morning. I couldn't help but wonder what was going through their minds as they tried to absorb all that had taken place. How does a six-year-old comprehend the loss of her mom? Can a nine-year-old truly grasp the meaning of death and life when death strikes so close?

The friends, family members, and neighbors in the room that day had all been touched by my wife, and they wanted to pay their respects for what she had meant to them. One friend from Nashville stood up and shared about the special relationship that he and his wife had enjoyed with us during our time at Forest Hills Baptist Church. Another person—a cousin of Sarah's—talked about her vibrant smile and warm personality.

The ripple-effect of Sarah's life was only beginning to be felt, but there was great peace to be gained from seeing the people in that room who knew and loved my wife, and hearing their loving tributes to her.

Afterwards, everyone gathered for lunch at a larger church nearby with a fellowship space that could accommodate all of the guests. As I visited with everyone, my spirits were lifted by the fact that so many people had made the time to come. Person after person stopped to say a few thoughtful words and hug my neck. Person after person assured us of their prayers and their support. But when it was over and everyone had gone home, I was done. I was so wiped out emotionally, spiritually, and physically that I went home, changed clothes, and crashed in my recliner.

That stupid chair. Just a week before it had been my place of comfort—the place where I unwound after busy days at work or long hours of yard work. It was there that I watched my favorite ballgames or enjoyed reruns of Disney classics as my children cuddled in my lap.

It was an old recliner—beat up, made of simple blue cloth, stained by my children when they couldn't hold down their formula (or by me, when I got careless with a game-day snack). It had always been a favorite place—a refuge—for me.

Just a few days after the accident, the doorbell interrupted one of the few quiet moments I'd had since my life had been turned upside down. I wasn't expecting anyone to drop by. Still, I crawled from that beat-up recliner—broken bones, sling, and all—and shuffled to the door, with my mom not far behind. I could make out the face of a young deliveryman in the glass panels surrounding the door. Surely this guy was lost. But when I opened the door, I saw that two men were standing there.

"Mr. Barron?" I was more than a little confused now because they had the correct name. "We've got something for you. Do you mind signing for it?"

Knowing I couldn't write with my broken wrist, Mom reached for the clipboard that they offered, hurriedly signed my name, and handed it back to the older of the two gentlemen.

"Where would you like it?" they asked. And then I saw it—sitting behind them on the front porch was a leather recliner. A very nice leather recliner. Though it was covered in plastic, and had a large tag hanging from one arm, I could see how nice the chair was.

"That's for me?" I still wasn't clear on what this was all about, but it sure looked promising.

"Yes, sir. It's a gift . . . from a friend."

As the two men hoisted the recliner and moved it to the spot where I pointed, I told them, "Just put it there, in the place of the blue one. I'll figure out what to do with that."

"We'll be glad to take it for you, Mr. Barron," they said. And without hesitating, they slid Old Blue out of its place and replaced it with the new leather recliner. Pulling a cutting device from his hip pocket, one of the guys rapidly slit open the plastic that surrounded the chair. He balled it quickly and placed it in the seat of the old recliner for disposal.

Still incredulous about what was happening, I queried, "Can I ask where it came from?"

Glancing down again at the clipboard, the older man said, "Sure. It's a friend of yours . . . a guy by the name of

Roberson. Robby Roberson." I smiled. Robby was another church member—one of those guys I loved hanging out with and had come to appreciate deeply as he and his family had gotten more involved in our congregation.

Now, my old friend—that blue recliner—had been traded out for a sleeker model. But it was no longer my friend as much as it was a constant reminder that life had changed.

With a broken shoulder, my doctors wouldn't allow me to lie down to sleep. So the recliner became my bed, my chair . . . and the crucible for my faith. Night after night for the next four months—often for hours on end—I would sit awake in that chair and scream and yell and whine at God. Though my physical body was debilitated, my heart and emotions and will were fully engaged in a wrestling match with the One who could have prevented the accident, but didn't.

It was there, in that chair, that I would go back to everything I had ever been taught by my parents. Every lesson I had learned in church was fair game. Every tenet of my faith was open to be challenged.

I questioned God, cried to Him—cried out to Him. Not just for me, but for my children.

Could it be that God was too small to handle my problems? Had He fallen asleep the day of the accident? Or had He just been looking the other way? Was it possible that God was punishing me for something I had or had not done?

There were times when I felt like I was losing my mind. But the nagging questions were not to be satisfied with the simple answers from my Sunday school days. What I was feeling called for something deeper—something that could only be pulled out by ongoing conversations with God and a lot of personal soul-searching. And that is exactly what comprised so many of my sleepless nights in that chair. But those four months—and the conclusions they would bring to me about the unending goodness of God and His unpredictable ways—would shape the years ahead for my children and me.

6

There is not much a man can do for himself when one shoulder is broken and the other wrist is fractured. Forget washing clothes or cleaning the house. Even shaving and putting on clothes become major tasks. Thankfully, my mother and my brother-in-law, Richard, stepped in to help with those responsibilities. Richard would wash my hair in the sink and shave me, then assist in bathing me as best as he and I could manage. It was absolutely one of the most humbling experiences I have ever been through. But his efforts were a true measure of love—as were my mom's sacrifices on behalf of the kids. She set aside her own loss and grief to help Harrison and Abby get ready for school each day, as well as doing laundry and keeping the house tidy. Without Richard and my mom, there is no way that even the smallest of things could have been handled in those first few weeks as I was learning to adapt to broken bones and the heartache of losing my wife.

At this same time, Keith and Tonda were helping me with Josh.

He had been transported to Memorial Hospital in Savannah, which was about three hours away. As soon as Tonda had checked on all of us to her satisfaction on the night of the accident, she had packed her suitcase and driven to Savannah to be at Josh's bedside through the weekend. She knew how important it was that there be a familiar face for him every time he would wake up. She bought him a new blanket and a little stuffed duck, all in an attempt to make him as comfortable as possible in that hospital room. She also frequently phoned me with updates on Josh's condition.

She stayed at his side till that Sunday afternoon, when she swapped places with a family friend (and another familiar face) so she could be home for the memorial service on Monday morning. But she didn't leave until the doctors had confirmed that Josh's condition was improving. In fact, they were hopeful he would not have to stay too long.

On Tuesday—the day after Sarah's memorial service in Douglas—I traveled to see Josh for the first time. Keith and Tonda drove me to the hospital. My mom and sister Harriet accompanied us, along with Sarah's mom, Sarah's sister, Tricia, and her husband, Neil. Sarah and I had always been very, very close to Tricia and Neil. Tricia was Sarah's best friend in the world, and I truly felt like Neil had been a brother almost from the time I'd met him thirteen years before.

Once at the hospital, we walked through the immaculately decorated lobby, down the maze of hallways, and up to the Pediatric Intensive Care Unit (PICU). Tonda guided me to a white phone on the wall just outside the double doors to the unit. I picked up the phone and was immediately greeted by a nurse's voice.

"My name is Ridley Barron," I said. "I'm here to see my son Josh."

"Yes, sir. Hold on just a minute, please."

It didn't take two seconds. The doors swung open immediately. We all entered the hallway, turned a corner, and walked into the first room on the right. It looked like most hospital rooms: on the wall opposite the large sliding glass door was Josh's bed; on the other side of the bed was a chair where our friend was sitting, along with several pieces of medical equipment that were alternately beeping and humming. The numbers that crossed the screen meant nothing to me. I just knew that their sounds meant my son was hanging in there.

However, nothing that Tonda had said over the weekend or on our trip to the hospital that morning had prepared me for this. I remember having this strange feeling as I walked into Josh's room. It all seemed so out of place—seeing my boy just lying there on that bed with tubes and wires attached to various parts of his tiny little body and his left arm raised up over his head. The wounds from the wreck were evident all over.

I was so stunned that I only took about three steps into the room and stopped, not sure what to do next. Tonda stepped closer to me and said, "Go over and talk to him, Ridley. It's okay." Then she moved around the foot of his bed to the other side.

The severity of his head wound caught me the most by surprise. *Poor guy,* I thought. *How do you explain to a seventeen-month-old why he feels so badly and why no one is making the pain go away?*

I hated seeing him that way. But I stepped up to Josh's bedside on his right, where I could more easily touch him. As I got closer, I realized he was still making that moaning noise, the one that I'd heard in the ambulance on the way to the hospital. I looked to Tonda, and she knew before I asked. "He's been doing that all weekend except when he's in deep sleep. He's just been very uncomfortable."

I moved in closer to his bed and placed my index finger into his tiny, half-curled right hand. His blond hair was matted to his head by some kind of cream the nurses had put on his head wound. His left eye was black and swollen. Around his left leg was a huge blue cuff for taking his blood pressure. And propped under Josh's left arm was the little duck that Keith and Tonda had bought him. There was a residue of tape around his mouth, but I could see that his lips were chapped and puffy. Leaning over the railing and closer to his ear, I whispered, "Hey, buddy, it's Daddy. It's okay, Joshie. I'm here, and it's going to be okay."

Instantly, the moan stopped. Josh gingerly rolled his head toward the sound of my voice. Tonda began to cry and exclaimed, "That's awesome, Ridley! It's the first time he's responded to anybody all weekend. He heard you!"

When Josh turned his head, I was able to see the severe grass burn on his left temple from where he'd slid across the ground after being thrown from the car. I could also see the beautiful blue of his eyes through his swollen black eye. I had joked for months that my son was going to drive the girls crazy with those eyes and his million-dollar smile. Yet in that moment, I couldn't raise a smile from him; his discomfort was too great. But the eyes were there, and I looked into them to reassure him that Daddy was going to take care of him.

There was an amazing nurse who carefully tended to Josh and us that entire day. When I began to cry, she offered me water and a wet compress. She respected our time with him and would regularly check to see if we needed anything in between her other duties. Then, at one point, she asked me if I would be interested in holding him. I jumped at the chance to do so.

"If you and the family will step outside, I'll take some of the equipment off so you can hold him. It will only be a second."

We were in the hall for no more than a minute or two when she pushed the curtain aside and urged me to come back in.

"Why don't you have a seat over there?" She motioned to the only chair in the room that occupied the small space between Josh's bed and a table against the wall. It was a beige chair with wooden trim, not meant for comfort or beauty, only convenience. "I'll bring him to you," she said.

The nurse laid Josh into my good arm as I propped my broken one on a pillow against the wooden arm. In our brief time out of the room, Josh's moaning had started again. But it quieted once more as he snuggled in close. I smelled his skin like I had a thousand times before—that unique smell that babies have. This time, though, that comforting smell was hindered by the odor of tape and gauze and medical creams that covered most of his body.

Despite all the obstacles, it was the first time Josh had seemed comfortable since we'd arrived. I held him and listened to his breathing as he labored to draw breath.

After about thirty minutes together, I gave him back to the nurse so she could lay him in the bed where he could rest. My family and I left to meet a friend for lunch and then returned to the hospital to visit with Josh for a few more minutes. We had to arrive back in Douglas that night so we could finalize plans for Sarah's transport to Franklin, Tennessee, where she would be buried. I also had a couple of doctor's appointments the following day.

Just before we were to leave and make the three-hour drive home, the nurse re-entered the room. "Mr. Barron, I know you and your family have to go back to Douglas tonight. I just wanted to check and see if there is anything else I can do for you before you leave."

"Yes," I told her. "I'd love to speak with the doctor who is in charge of Josh's care. I really haven't had a chance to talk to him yet."

She nodded her head and disappeared for a few minutes before returning to the room. "If you'll pick up the phone on the other side of the bed, Mr. Barron, the doctor is on the line." She motioned to a simple white handset on the table next to the chair where I had sat earlier. "He's currently making rounds at other hospitals and won't be able to get back here before you and your family leave," she continued. "But he definitely wants to speak with you."

Though Josh's doctor and I were on the phone only briefly, we talked candidly about his head injury—which was the biggest concern. I asked about the severity of it.

"Well, it's kind of hard to say," the doctor admitted. "Unfortunately, with children who are Josh's age, we can't get feedback from the patient regarding the level of their pain or how they are feeling. So we pretty much have to rely on the battery of tests and scans that we have done. On his MRI we can see that he had a pretty severe head injury after being thrown from the vehicle. Since he arrived here Friday evening, Josh has had several seizures as a direct result of the injury. Each time, our nurses have administered phenytoin [a form of the popular anti-seizure medication known as Dilantin]. And each time, Josh has responded favorably, with his condition returning to normal."

"Okay, that leads to my next question," I said. "On Thursday, our family will be flying his mother to Middle Tennessee for her burial. Is there any chance at all that his condition will improve to the point where he could fly with us and be a part of it?"

The doctor hesitated. "Mr. Barron, it's hard to say with a child Josh's age. We just don't know the extent of his injury. However, based on what I saw this weekend and what I am hearing from the nurses this afternoon, I feel like there is a chance that he will be able to travel with you on Thursday."

As we ended the call, he apologized again for not being able to be there in person to talk with us. I thanked him for his time and for all he was doing for my son. We then said good-bye to Josh and to our friend Helen, who was staying at Josh's side through the night, and my family and I got back into the car to return to Douglas.

7

April fourteenth dawned with the heat of a spring day in South Georgia, announcing that summer was soon to arrive. It was Wednesday, only five days after the accident. It seemed like months.

That morning, Tonda and I were running a few errands to prepare for our trip north for Sarah Ellen's burial. While I had the responsibility of seeing to the details in Franklin, Tennessee, my mind was fixed on a hospital bed in Savannah, Georgia, where my toddler still lay.

I was emotionally, mentally, and physically drained as we got in and out of the car, errand after errand. Tonda and I chatted a little, but I was still stunned about all that was going on. Too stunned to carry on any lengthy conversation.

About mid-morning, Tonda's cell phone rang. At the other end of the call was Helen, our friend. I could only hear Tonda's end of the conversation, but I could tell it wasn't good.

"Why did they make you leave, Helen? . . . They aren't telling you anything? . . . How long has it been?" With each question, Tonda's voice grew more desperate.

Before she could finish her phone call, my cell phone buzzed. I answered, "This is Ridley."

"Mr. Barron?" The woman gave her name and introduced herself. "I am a nurse from Memorial in Savannah," she began. "I need to see if there is any way you could return to the hospital."

"Ma'am, can you tell me what's going on?" I asked.

"No, sir. HIPAA regulations won't allow me to tell you anything beyond the fact that we'd like you to come back to the hospital." (HIPAA stands for the Health Insurance Portability and Accountability Act, a law that assures that all patients have a right to privacy.) She seemed very agitated. I was feeling agitated too.

"I understand, ma'am, but I'm not just around the corner in Savannah. I am almost three hours away. If this is because a doctor wants to speak with me or something of that nature, can I come later this afternoon or speak with him by phone?"

"Sir, I really can't tell you more due to HIPAA concerns."

I was getting furious. "Ma'am, I understand that. But you called *me*! You know who I am! Can't you tell me anything?"

The click at the other end was deafening. Had she really just hung up on me?

I immediately hit the callback button and hurriedly filled Tonda in while I waited for someone to pick up. "She didn't give me any information, Tonda. What did Helen tell you?"

Before she could reply, a nurse answered my call. I launched in right away. "Can I speak to the head nurse?!"

"Yes, please hold." *Hold? She wants me to hold?*

With every second that passed, my fears and my anger grew.

The head nurse came on, and before she could introduce herself, I jumped in. "Ma'am, I just received a very cryptic phone call from one of your people. She asked if I could come to the hospital. I'm three hours away. Is—is this something important? An emergency or something? Can you tell me more?" I don't even know if what I said made any sense, I was stammering so much.

"Sir, I can tell you that whatever you are doing, you should drop it. You and your family need to make your way to Savannah as quickly and as safely as possible."

"Is there anything I ought to know?"

"Just come," was her reply.

Though I was at a loss about what was going on, I was clear about what needed to happen next: we had to get back to Savannah. Now.

Tonda called Keith immediately and we figured out the plan: she and I would ride with Keith in his truck.

We made the three-hour journey in about two and a half hours and then rushed back to the Pediatric Intensive Care Unit as soon as we arrived at the hospital. Tonda reached for the white phone, just as we had the day before.

"Mr. Barron is here to see his son Josh."

"The father is out there?" the nurse asked.

"Yes," Tonda answered.

"Just one moment. We'll be right out." There was a slight delay as the nurse whispered something inaudible to someone standing nearby.

The doors stayed closed. I looked nervously at Tonda, Keith, and Helen, who had now joined us. Helen was telling us that she had been begging for answers for the last two hours, but no one would tell her anything.

After what seemed like an eternity, the doors swung open. But before we could make our way into the hallway leading to Josh's room, we were intercepted by a group of people, their badges and stethoscopes indicating that they were doctors and hospital administrators.

The guy in the lead asked, "Mr. Barron, can you and the rest of your family join us across the hall in this conference room?" He motioned to a single wooden door that was opposite the PICU phone.

After the last person entered and my family was seated, the man who seemed to be the spokesman for the group turned and closed the door. The entire hospital group continued to stand.

Clearing his throat, the doctor began, "Mr. Barron, there has been a horrible mistake . . ."

I never heard anything else the man said. I don't even know how long we sat in that room or what else was talked about. My mind just shut down.

When the first man finished, another gentleman—the

vice president for risk management—asked, "Mr. Barron, is there anything at all we can do for you?"

I looked up at him, unsure of what was happening. I said the only thing a daddy knows to say in that situation. "Can I see my son?"

He nodded, adding, "Can you give us just a second?"

Someone—I forget who—soon returned to the hallway to tell us they were ready. We walked toward Josh's room. I turned the corner, stepped just inside the door, and stopped where I had the day before. Only this time, the scene was entirely different.

The day before, Josh had been lying in his bed, one arm slung up over his head on the pillow. He'd had tubes and monitors attached to different places on his body. He had moaned and fidgeted with a restless discomfort. Today, a sheet was covering most of his body, and on the far side of the bed was a group of doctors and nurses all gathered around with worried looks on their faces while one woman stood over Josh's bed, very intent on some task that I couldn't see. The medical staff watched me as I entered the room, and I remember thinking they all looked like they had been caught doing something wrong. I guess, in some way, they had. I just didn't understand what all of this was about.

When I walked in from the hallway, the same risk-management executive who had spoken up in the conference room approached me. I would later be told that his name was Wayne Marchant.

"Mr. Barron?"

I cringed. Every time they called me that name, it seemed to be followed by some really bad news.

I turned to face him.

"Mr. Barron," he said again. "We need to know what you want us to do."

"What I want you to do?" I asked, stupefied. "I don't even know what's going on here! Who are these people, and what's happening to my son?"

Pointing to the lady on the other side of the bed, he said, "She is a pediatric cardiologist. This morning, your son had another seizure related to his head injury. We ordered phenytoin from the pharmacy downstairs to stop the seizure. This particular medication had always worked before. This time, however, the pharmacist downstairs made an error in medication and sent up an adult dosage—five times the strength that is required. She forgot to dilute it for Josh. And the nurse who administered it didn't catch it.

"This particular medication is like superglue in the veins," he continued. "Once administered, there's nothing we can do to counteract it. We cannot induce vomiting, administer charcoal—none of the typical procedures that usually help in these instances. When the phenytoin was given, Josh's heart stopped immediately."

I pointed to the pediatric cardiologist who was still standing over Josh's bed. "What is she doing?" I asked.

"That woman, Mr. Barron, has her hands inside your son's chest. She has been massaging his heart to keep him alive until you got here."

I was shocked, devastated, and incredulous—all at the same time.

"Are you telling me that her hand inside my son's chest is the only thing keeping him alive?" The words didn't even sound right coming out of my mouth. I hoped I had completely misunderstood everything he said.

Mr. Marchant glanced around at his peers before answering. "Sir, in all likelihood, if the doctor removes her hand from your son's chest, he will pass away."

I had never really liked that term *pass away*. Ever. Right then, I hated it.

I felt like someone had punched me in the gut. I kept thinking, *Not this. Not now. After all that has happened to us already, couldn't God have spared me this one thing?* And yet there was only one thing to do. One agonizing thing that no parent should ever have to do.

"Then let him go," I whispered.

"Sir?" he repleied, wanting to make sure he'd heard my words. "Are you saying you want the doctor to stop?"

"I'm saying let him go." Reasoning in that fuzzy moment that his mom must obviously want Josh in heaven with her, I felt I had to let him go. My baby had already been through so much; I didn't want him to suffer.

The doctor who had been massaging Josh's heart looked up at me. Slowly she removed her hand from his chest cavity. Moving away from the edge of the bed, she took a towel and wiped the blood from her hands.

Careful, lady, I thought to myself. *That's my son's blood.* In retrospect, I don't even know what I meant by that. I just remember thinking it.

As she moved away, she said, "Mr. Barron, you can speak to him. He can still hear you."

I stepped forward, leaning closer to Josh's head. I found myself in the same place I had been about twenty-four hours earlier, on my first visit. Josh's eyes were closed, but I hoped that maybe he could hear me or even smell me one more time before his soul left his body.

With every sob, my chest felt like my lungs were going to explode. "Josh," I began, not sure if I really believed the doctor but too afraid not to at least try, "I love you, buddy. Daddy loves you a lot. You go be with Mommy, okay? She's there, and she's waiting for you. When I get there, I'm going to get your mama. She must have convinced God she needed you there worse than I needed you here."

It was a poor attempt to diffuse the pain, but I had to do something; I was just hurting so much inside.

Then . . . *silence,* followed by the sound of muted sniffling. I straightened up and turned to face Mr. Marchant again. Over his left shoulder, I saw the nurse who had cared for

Josh during a large portion of his stay. Tears filled her eyes. She returned my gaze and then silently left the room.

"Mr. Barron," Marchant spoke, "would you like to hold your son one more time?"

"Yes, I'd like that."

"Why don't you step outside and let us remove the medical equipment? We'll get him cleaned up and ready for you. I'll come and get you as soon as we're ready."

I stepped from the room with my sister at my side. Keith joined us as we returned to the conference room where the doctors had broken the news to me. We whispered about all that was going on, still in shock from what the doctors had told us and the scene that had just played out in Josh's room. A few minutes later, the door to the room eased open. It was a nurse, coming to let me know that Josh was ready.

I walked back down the hallway to his room. Easing myself into the chair where I had held Josh the day before, I prepared for his body to be placed into my good arm. Gently, the nurse laid Josh's lifeless form into the crook of my arm. I couldn't believe it—his body was cold, empty, only a shadow of the life it once held. Josh was gone.

This is not my son, I thought to myself.

I was done. I knew with all my heart that Josh was with his mom and with Jesus, far away from the flesh-and-bone that lay in my lap.

I looked up at the nurse, who was standing nearby. "You can take him; he's not here anymore. He's already Home."

8

While I was holding Josh for the last time, Keith was huddling with administrators and doctors in the hallway, continuing the conversation that had begun in the conference room and trying to get to the bottom of what had happened. Finally, Keith interrupted the discussion: "Gentlemen, I truly appreciate your candor. The nature with which you've dealt with my brother-in-law and our family is to be commended. Because you have been so transparent about things, I think it is only fair that I do the same for you: I am a lawyer, and I specialize in medical malpractice."

Feel free to laugh; I did later when he shared this part of the story with me. At this point—perhaps not so surprisingly—every one of those men excused themselves and walked away, with the exception of one. Looking around to see if the others were out of earshot, he stepped closer to Keith and said softly, "Sir, I am telling you that the hospital has made a horrible mistake. You do what you must to take care of Mr. Barron and his family."

Our journey home that afternoon felt completely different than the one the day before. Instead of anticipation about Josh's progress, there was heaviness. Disbelief. And another level of sadness I had never felt.

As we rode in the truck, we couldn't help but talk about what had happened. We talked about the hospital's responsibilities and how I should respond. Although Keith was usually on the other side of such events—representing the hospitals and doctors—he had agreed to help me navigate the legal journey that lay ahead.

After listening to everyone's input, I finally spoke up. There was a world of things that I wasn't sure about in all of this—a world of things I couldn't control—but one decision seemed clear: I could decide how I wanted to respond to what had happened. And so I did.

"Keith, I want two things communicated to the hospital. First, I want them to tell the pharmacist who made the mistake that I forgive her. She very well may have been the one that kept my son alive the first four days with her talents. She had no ill will, and there was no deliberate negligence on her part. Please make sure they let her know that I hold no bitterness toward her."

Keith nodded. "Secondly, I want you to communicate to them that—because of who I am and what I believe—I'm not going to be like everybody else and sue them to get rich off of their mistake. It is just that . . . a mistake. I do think they owe me some kind of compensation for what has happened. But I don't want to sue them. You okay with that?"

Again, Keith nodded. "I'll make sure to communicate those things to them first thing tomorrow when I talk to them," he said.

Looking back, I can see that this difficult choice has made a great deal of difference. Others have told me that they believe this was *the* true turning point for me and my family—the choice that paved the way for everything that followed. I'm not God, so I don't have the whole picture. But what I do know is that when life doesn't turn out the way we planned, we are either going to sow bitterness and misery, or forgiveness and grace. And what we sow, we ultimately reap in return.

However, in that moment, during that sobering ride home from the hospital, I had no idea of the long-term results of this decision. I was just trying to get through the next hour—and the one after that, and the one that followed—and do what I believed to be right.

Once I had communicated my wishes, my thoughts turned to Abby and Harrison. I knew there was no way I could hide this from them; they would see it in my face. As a minister, I had delivered this kind of bad news before, but never to someone in my own family—and never to anyone under the age of fifteen.

How in the world would my kids handle this kind of news after losing their mom? I had promised I would take care of them; I had prayed for these kids, protected these kids, and taught them how to be safe; I would have gladly given my life for any one of them. And yet Josh was dead, and I hadn't been able to prevent it. How would Abby and Harrison ever believe my words again? I felt like I had let all three of my kids down.

The closer we got to the house, the sicker I felt.

This time, when I walked into the house, I noticed how quiet it was. Not a peaceful quiet or the kind that makes you feel rested. It was a quiet like someone had sucked the life out of the walls. Sarah was not in her familiar place, cooking a delicious meal for the family that she loved so deeply. Josh's thousand-watt smile was no longer lighting up the place. And while Harrison and Abby were occupied with playing, it was not the joyful, carefree play of children. In less than a week, everything about our family had changed, and there was no going back.

Knowing I needed to sit down with the kids before they got wind of what had happened to Josh, I asked Abby and Harrison to come into my room. They joined me on the far side of the bed on the floor. The youthful energy that had filled their faces only a few days before seemed to be gone. I thought to myself, *How much can two little kids take? Haven't they been through enough?*

My own childhood seemed so sheltered in comparison: No one ever died until they were really old. No one ever got divorced or ran away or had horrible accidents. I don't even remember hearing the word *cancer* until I was in high school. I'm sure that people were suffering around me; nevertheless, I was shielded from it, as any parent wants their children to be.

Now, though, I was preparing to share bad news with my kids for the second time in just five days. They had felt a lifetime of hurt since Friday afternoon. Could they take much more?

I wasn't sure how to begin, so I just took a breath and tried to find a way, hoping the words wouldn't feel as awkward to the kids as they did to me.

"You know Daddy had to go back over to the hospital in Savannah today where Josh was, right?" I began to cry, my face twisting as I tried to hold back my emotions. Abby edged closer in my lap while Harrison pulled back to get a better look at me. "What's wrong, Daddy?" he asked.

"Well, guys, the doctors made a little mistake and gave Josh too much of his medicine." I paused to see if it was sinking in. It was. "Josh is dead. He's gone to be where Mommy is and keep her company."

"We're not going to see him any more." Abby was half asking, half making a statement as her blue eyes began to puddle for the thousandth time since the accident.

"No, baby, we aren't. Josh is in heaven with Mommy right now. He is with her in heaven, and it's just the three of us."

Both of them were buried in my chest now. Harrison didn't cry much. I think he had become numb to bad news by this point. Still, you could see the sadness written all over his little face, his forehead wrinkling tightly as he held back what was inside. He began to rub his forehead as he had done many times over the past five days.

I let them both sit for a few minutes in the silence, and then I pulled them off of my lap and put them in front of me so I could look them square in the face.

"I need both of you to listen to me for a minute," I said gently. "For as long as you live, you have my permission to get upset about this, okay? You can cry; you can get angry; we can talk about this anytime you want, and you can ask any questions you like. Those things are always okay. Understand?"

Both of them nodded. I wondered if they really did understand. But the months ahead would prove that this conversation helped a great deal as we sought to rebuild our lives.

It was essential that all three of us have a place where we could hurt and grieve. It was the only way we could ever hope to begin healing.

9

On the morning of Friday, April 16, I woke with a start. My body was stiff and racked with pain—still. I wondered, *How long can I hurt like this?* It had been a week since the accident, but the physical effects were ever present. I struggled to ease myself out of the recliner in my hotel room. *Not quite as comfy as the leather one back home,* I thought.

That morning in Brentwood, Tennessee—the morning of Sarah and Josh's funeral—was bright and sunny. The night before, our family had arrived in Middle Tennessee. It was the place where Sarah Ellen and I had served for over six years in student ministry. The place we had both felt God calling us to return to in order to plant a new church.

As the kids and I had been welcomed back by dozens of friends at dinner the previous evening, we had all talked about our memories. Though I would've given almost anything to change the circumstances, it was good to get caught up with former students and their parents. It was also good to be back "home." I knew with all my heart that this is where Sarah wanted to be buried, and I felt relieved to have the support of so many friends.

In the bedroom of our hotel suite, Abby was still sleeping. I laughed to myself, realizing I would never forget what Sarah Ellen was like as long as Abby lives. She is truly the image of her mother. Standing there beside Abby's bed, I think I realized how much that is true for the first time. She has Sarah's crooked little smile that popped up on her face so easily. She also has Sarah's personality and her long, lean frame. Leaning over, I kissed her on the forehead and told her it was time to get ready.

Once I woke up Harrison too, the three of us cleaned up and got dressed for the funeral. My brother-in-law, Richard, helped me finish getting ready. Then our family made its way to the lobby to grab breakfast.

The funeral was not far off now. I remember thinking how surreal everything was. If not for the sling around my shoulder, I would have sworn that this was all for someone else—that Sarah and Josh were simply still up in the room and would be joining us any minute.

Friends who had arrived overnight were gathering in the lobby of the hotel. Few knew how to act. Are there really any right words to say on such an occasion? I tried my best to put each of them at ease. Lord knows I had attended my share of funerals where nothing seemed appropriate to offer as conversation.

As we finished the last bites of breakfast, gentlemen from the funeral home arrived to walk us through the schedule for the morning. It was a celebration befitting the life of a woman who had given her all for Christ. The service was filled with praise music and tributes to Sarah Ellen's character. Several hundred people had gathered to say their good-byes to my wife and a child that many of them had never met. There were more tributes from close friends and a song sung by one of our former students in the youth ministry. The choir at Forest Hills Baptist Church gave their best in tribute to Sarah and offered praise to God for her life.

Throughout the service, Abby and Harrison sat tightly up against me. I alternated between tears of fear and sorrow, joy and anger. From time to time I stopped to place my good arm around both of the kids and to pray silently that God was healing them already and preparing them for what lay ahead. I prayed for myself as well. This first week had been a personal hell for me. The emotional roller coaster was taking its toll. There were small victories and overwhelming acts of love shown to us. But no matter how many of those encouragements were heaped on us, nothing could diminish the loss of my best friend and my precious child.

The graveside service was brief. Although it was April, the weather was brisk and a little windy. I laughed when I took my appointed seat beside Josh and Sarah Ellen's graves, because across the road, work was being completed on a new Target shopping center. I leaned over to Sarah Ellen's mother and whispered, "This is just like your daughter; she'd do anything to get to a Target." Mrs. Trimble chuckled and nodded her head in agreement.

After the graveside ceremony, hundreds of people reconvened at the church for lunch. Churchgoing people sure like to eat. If not for the tears and the somber reminders, it could have been a reunion, given how many familiar faces were there. I tried to spend some time with each person and let them know how much it meant that they had given their Friday to be a part of this.

A few hours later, the family and I were on a plane headed back to Douglas, Georgia. An organization known as Angel Flight had agreed, as part of their ministry, to fly us for free to ease the burden we were under. (Way to go, guys! You were awesome.) If my memory serves me, it was on that flight that I broke the news to my sister and her family that we would probably be leaving Douglas to return to Franklin. I remember that neither Keith nor Tonda seemed surprised.

Talk was minimal for most of the flight, but my mind was consumed with thoughts about the future. At best, I was uncertain. I didn't know what I would do or how I would respond emotionally and spiritually to the challenges that were to come, so I laid my head back against the headrest and began to pray. These had to be some of the funniest prayers I've ever uttered . . .

"God, can You help me handle the laundry?"

"I'm not exactly sure how to do Abby's hair, God. I think I can handle a ponytail, but how long can a little girl go with a ponytail?"

"What in the heck am I going to do about cooking for these two?"

The next four months were nothing but a roller-coaster spiritual journey. In spite of the fancy new recliner I'd been given, sleep seldom came easily, thanks to my broken shoulder—and even more so, my broken spirit. There were many restless nights as my soul continued to wrestle with God. I couldn't wrap my mind around why this had happened and how it could possibly be a part of God's plan. The nights were filled with thousands and thousands of tears. My heart would waiver between determined confidence in God and flickers of doubt. Literally everything I had believed to this point was placed on the table to be examined . . . questioned . . . challenged. I asked God to heal me, fix me, save me, prove Himself to me. And sometimes I asked Him to leave me alone. And yet, night after night, I kept talking with Him—crying out to Him so loudly that at times I was sure I would wake everyone in the house.

He and I continued to debate, just as the Bible's Job had done. I questioned. I complained. I pitied myself. Sometimes I would find that I was so mad that I couldn't even think of anything to say. Then one night, I finally admitted, "For crying out loud, God, I work for You and this is the best I get?"

Realizing the absurdity of what I'd just said, I laughed at myself. "It's okay," I cajoled. "I have been through a lot, so it's okay to be stupid. Just don't let anyone hear me."

It was not my finest moment. And yet in the honesty of it, I realized something important: slowly, almost imperceptibly, my lost and shaken faith was being restored and I could feel myself being drawn closer and closer to this God who had seemed like a stranger since the accident.

It ended up being a stepping-stone toward a different kind of normal.

10

My mother continued to help with the household necessities—the laundry, the cleaning, tending to my kids when I couldn't. Looking back, I realize how much she took upon herself only two short months after Dad died. Forty-plus years of marriage had come to an end for her, and now, before she could process her own grief, more sadness had been added to her heart. She was a trooper through it all. Yet I resented the need for help some days.

In a strange way, Mom's presence made me feel like a child again; it reminded me of my inability to handle things myself. I hated that my kids couldn't count on me for certain stuff, and that my mother (seventy years old at the time) had to do for them what their daddy should be doing. At least while Mom was staying with us, she never had to prepare a dinner. The church I served, and the friends we had in the little town where we lived, responded in a way I had never seen. For the first four months after the accident, they prepared every dinner for me and my family. That was an incredible gesture of love and care.

One thing I *could* do for my kids was be available to talk, and I tried my best. One night, as I was tucking the kids into bed and praying with them, I laid down with Abby for a few minutes. She was only six at the time, but old enough to comprehend some of the drastic changes that our life might call for. As we finished praying, she looked up at me with those big, blue eyes and asked, "Daddy, are you going to find us another mom?"

This wasn't the first time she'd asked. Harrison had similar questions. It was not an insult to me or to their mother, for they weren't looking to replace Sarah Ellen. Instead, in the innocence of childhood, they simply wanted to regain the stability that had seemed in doubt since the accident. They wanted back the one thing that would seem to fix it—a mother.

I chuckled to myself when Abby asked the question, though I was careful not to make her feel weird for asking. She made it sound like I could run down to the local department store and try on another wife for size. All I could answer was, "Maybe"—unsure if my answer was a good one or even the right one. "That really depends on God, baby. But you and I can ask Him to help us."

"Why just 'maybe'? Do you want to get married again?" She was genuinely perplexed that my answer had not been more certain or positive.

"It's going to depend on a lot of things," I explained. "You have to understand that guys like Daddy aren't in big demand."

Even in the dim light, I could see the confusion on her face, so I continued. "Not very many women are looking for someone like me . . . I'm thirty-six years old, have two kids, and I'm a pastor. Not exactly things that top most women's search list."

Content that I was getting through to her, I bent over to kiss her good night. Her next words will probably be engraved on my heart for the rest of my life. They are the kind that steal a daddy's heart: "I'd marry you, Daddy. I think you're pretty."

I laughed as I slipped from the room and headed for my recliner. But her questions had caused me to think. *What would the future hold? Did I really want to get married again? Was there something—someone—that could fill the void that I felt over losing my best friend?*

11

The kids and I pushed forward with life as close to normal as we could. I wanted Abby and Harrison to feel the changes as little as possible, so the week after the accident, Harrison was back on the baseball field and I was in my familiar place in the dugout as his coach. We finished that season in first place. It was a small lift to two hearts that had been hurt so deeply.

I'll never forget the night that Harrison drove in the winning run with a bases-loaded bunt. For months, he and I had been working on bunting in the back yard. When that run crossed the plate during the ballgame, I searched the field to try and catch his eye. I know this may sound funny, but his look of excitement was just one of the small ways that God was saying to me—"Yes, things can be 'normal' again." It was just going to be a new kind of normal for us.

In late spring, Keith and Tonda traveled with me to Savannah to have our first meeting with the lawyers and administrators representing the hospital. I was as nervous as I could be because I had no idea what to expect. Keith and Tonda's presence comforted me, but I was still very intimidated about talking with these people about such a subject. My nervousness would turn to anger and outrage once the hospital's legal strategy became apparent. Their attorney was saying Josh probably would have died from his head injury anyway. At the very least, they were going to attempt to prove that, if Josh had lived, he would have been nothing more than a vegetable who would never have advanced very far developmentally, would not have been able to receive much of an education, and would have brought limited income to our family in future years.

After several hours of listening to their attempts to measure the financial value of my son's life, I was tired and frustrated. The tone and tension of the conversation was wearing on what little patience I had left. I remember saying to them at one point, "I told you earlier that, because of my faith, I did not want to sue you guys for this tragic mistake. However, if this conversation doesn't change its course, I can ignore my faith for just a little while. I will sue you and . . ." I was so flustered I could hardly speak.

"You keep talking about my son in terms of how much he would make for our family, as if he were some kind of investment! I tell you, my son lit up my world every time he smiled. Every time he came into the room, he was worth a million dollars to me. Keep it up and you will be paying me more than you imagined!"

There were constant references to my son as a "sentinel event"—medical terminology for an adverse outcome caused by hospital error. The lawyers and administrators were using charts and MRI scans and numbers and statistics to make their point. But the more they did this, the madder I got, because they were missing the *real* point: this wasn't just a medical case with a number and statistics.

Having had enough, I slapped my hand down on the table and said, "My son is not a sentinel event! He is a child!" I turned to Keith directly and added, "You know all that crap I said about being a Christian and not suing them? Just forget it. I'm tired of this."

Keith saved me from myself by bringing a quick end to the day's meetings.

I was beside myself. Several hours later, we were no closer to a resolution than we'd been when we started that morning. Yet even then, God was up to something behind the scenes, because that day I crossed paths with two men who would help the promise of Romans 8:28—"All things work together for good for those who love the Lord and are called according to his purpose"—come true in my life: Bill Franklin, the head lawyer representing the hospital; and Wayne Marchant, the hospital's vice president of risk management who had been by my side the day Josh died. Both men were believers and, although none of us could imagine how, our paths would intersect in some key ways in the days ahead.

In June, I had the pleasure of baptizing Abby in a cow trough just outside our little church. Sarah Ellen had had the pleasure of watching Abby give her life to follow Christ just before the accident. The day of Abby's baptism, I cried because Sarah had to watch this part from heaven. I knew she would have been beaming had she been there. Abby sure was.

Then came a monumental moment a few weeks later. During one of my late-night conversations with God, I was in my recliner looking out the back window of our home. The July moon was full and amazingly bright that night. Despite the tears that filled my eyes, I could make out the details of the play set in our back yard and the details of the neighbor's house in the distance. It was a dark moment, probably one of the darker ones I'd had. My feelings were in direct contrast to the moonlight that literally streamed in through the blinds of my house. I was emotionally exhausted, walking a thin line between the faith I had held for years and the doubts that were swirling in my head. Every time I found peace, it seemed some other question would stir me up again.

Quietly, I spoke with God. "God, I don't know that I can do this. I'm tired and scared. I'm so lonely and afraid of what I don't know is out there." I paused to think about the words. I don't know if I was just thinking them in my head or actually saying them out loud, but I continued: "I want to make a deal with You. If You will promise to go with me, I'll go wherever You want me to go, say whatever You want me to say. You just have to promise that You will bring good out of Sarah and Josh's death."

I didn't know how God might answer that prayer, but I felt compelled to trust that He would. And at the very least, I felt better.

Only time would tell what God was up to.

12

It was mid-July when I announced to my congregation in Georgia that our family would be moving back to Franklin, Tennessee, at the end of the month to start a new church there. We were returning to Middle Tennessee at the request of our former church, Forest Hills Baptist, to begin a new work in the area.

It was a very difficult decision that was made harder because of the way our church family in Douglas had loved on us since April. More than just meals, there were cards, phone calls, visits, yards cut, bushes trimmed, and special attention paid to the needs of my kids. Still, the kids and I were excited about the chance to return to Franklin. Both of them had been born there, and there was a sense in which they were going home.

In early July, just before my announcement to the Douglas congregation, I had stopped off in Nashville on the way to speak at a friend's summer youth camp. He was bringing his youth group from Indiana to East Tennessee. During that trip I had picked out a house that seemed perfect for us. It was a five-bedroom place, much bigger than our needs at the time, but God had put it on my heart to buy that house, believing that I would be married again someday—and that the woman I married would likely have children of her own.

The house was just around the corner from the school where our church would meet. It was also across the street from the soccer and baseball complexes where the kids and I would spend many of our Saturdays in the spring and fall. It also sat on a popular walking and running path that many people in our area used.

Speaking at the camp had been on the calendar long before the accident. After the accident, Toby—my youth minister friend—had called. "Listen, Ridley, after all that's gone on, are you sure you still want to do this? I can find someone else to be our camp pastor. If nothing else, I can lead it."

I really didn't have to think about it. I had tried very hard to get the kids back into the routines of life, to remind them that their lives would still go on. Harrison picked right back up with baseball and school. Abby did the same with her friends and other interests. I felt like Toby's camp was my way to continue to move forward and seek to regain some form of normal.

"Yes. I'm sure, Toby. I really appreciate you asking and being sensitive, but I need to do this for you . . . and for me."

So, I found myself with Toby and his kids—a great group of youth I had led in past years. Only, the last time I was with them, Sarah was with me.

The second night of camp, I had just finished speaking to the kids. As the worship team took their places to close out the evening meeting, I was half paying attention, half thinking about where the past few months had taken me. The leader said, "I want to introduce you to a new song we're doing. I think you'll like it; it has some really meaningful words."

It was certainly the first time I had heard the song, but it wouldn't be the last. It became a powerful anthem for me amid all I was learning and all that God was doing in me.

Blessed be Your name
In the land that is plentiful
Where Your streams of abundance flow
Blessed be Your name

Blessed be Your name
When I'm found in the desert place
Though I walk through the wilderness
Blessed be Your name

Every blessing You pour out
I'll turn back to praise
When the darkness closes in, Lord
Still I will say

Blessed be the name of the Lord
Blessed be Your name
Blessed be the name of the Lord
Blessed be Your glorious name

As the lyrics hit my ears, my heart was leaping inside of me. Somehow those words were capturing everything I was feeling at that moment. I turned my face toward the sky and began to sing with all my heart. The tears were streaming down my face. I felt as if brick after brick was being removed from my shoulders.

I had prayed for months on end, "God, show me You are still there. Show me what You are up to and how I can be a part of it. Show me what faith is like when my world has fallen apart." Here was His answer in the form of a song. The band continued as I worshiped:

Blessed be Your name
When the sun's shining down on me
When the world's all as it should be
Blessed be Your name

Blessed be Your name
On the road marked with suffering
Though there's pain in the offering
Blessed be Your name

Every blessing You pour out
I'll turn back to praise
When the darkness closes in, Lord
Still I will say

Blessed be the name of the Lord
Blessed be Your name

Blessed be the name of the Lord
Blessed be Your glorious name

You give and take away
You give and take away
My heart will choose to say
Lord, blessed be Your name[2]

In August, after that camp experience, I busied myself with the work of church planting—meeting with members of the core group who would help get the church established later that month—and investing extra time into Harrison and Abby to help ease the loss of their mother. My job gave me the freedom to make all of their games and practices, programs and class parties. I was "Mr. Mom" to the *nth* degree. I wasn't always comfortable in that role, but I felt a strong desire to do everything I could so my kids knew I was there.

I remember the first time I showed up at a class party. Around the room was mother after mother . . . and me. As I walked in the room, I was greeted with skeptical smiles and a few awkward exchanges. I tried my best to focus on serving and not draw attention to myself. Mostly, though, those first few times, I stood off to the side and moved only when asked to. I wasn't exactly sure what a single dad was supposed to do.

In late September, I received the latest phone call from Keith regarding the legal issues with the hospital that still hung ominously over my family. Keith and my sister had moved to Franklin just a few weeks after the kids and I had settled in. They felt very strongly that their family needed to be in Franklin with us—to help us with the church, to help me with my kids, and to give their family a fresh start.

In this call, Keith said Mr. Franklin and Mr. Marchant were ready to sit down with us again. They would be in Nashville in October and wanted to know if we could take the time to meet. My instinct was to say no. I didn't want to go through the whole "sentinel event" conversation again. It had hurt so badly the first time that I had no desire to expose myself to that kind of talk anymore. But I also knew that such conversations had to happen to bring a resolution to it all.

By the time that meeting took place in October, I had prayed over and over about how it would unfold. I was attempting to walk a fine line. On one side was the Christ follower I wanted to be, showing grace and understanding without rolling over and playing dead. On the other side was a human being—hurt by the loss of his wife and son—who wanted someone to pay, and to pay very dearly, for what they had done.

I knew what was right. I also knew which was easier.

I arrived at Keith's office in downtown Nashville a few

minutes early to make sure that everything was okay and to settle into my chair before the two gentlemen from Savannah arrived. Cordial greetings were passed around when Mr. Franklin and Mr. Marchant got there, and we jumped right into the issue at hand.

Wayne Marchant began by apologizing yet again for the horrible error that the hospital made that day. He even went one step farther and apologized for the course the previous meeting had taken and the way it had ended. He mentioned that he and Bill (Mr. Franklin) were both men of faith and had respected my response to the circumstances surrounding Josh's death. Now I was seeing it: God was obviously behind this meeting and working through the conversation.

As a result, what we could not accomplish in half a day earlier that spring was completed in a little over thirty minutes that morning several months later. After I had signed the last of the documents regarding the settlement, I slid the stack of papers back across the table to Mr. Franklin.

Mr. Marchant cleared his throat and began to speak softly: "Ridley, I have said how thankful the hospital is for the way in which you have handled yourself in regards to our error. I am going to apologize in advance for what I am about to ask, because there is really no good way to say it." He hesitated, and then continued, "I was wondering if you would be willing to come back to the hospital and speak to our staff. You see, they are used to numbers and graphs and charts and statistics regarding these kinds of events. Your willingness to come and speak would put a face on this kind of tragedy, make it more personal for our people."

I smiled. God is so good! My mind immediately flashed back to that summer night in Douglas, sitting awake in that recliner. I remembered my tears and my confused words to God there in the darkness. And . . . I remembered the deal I had made with Him. Once again, God had shown that He never fails to keep His end of the promise.

I chuckled as I began, "Mr. Marchant, I would love to do that . . . Let me tell you about a deal I made with God."

We finished our conversation that day with the four of us enjoying lunch at a local restaurant and praying together over that meal.

13

In December of 2004, just eight months after the accident, I found myself in Savannah at the hospital where Josh had died. At Wayne Marchant's request, I was being given an opportunity to speak at their Grand Rounds. This continuing education opportunity would provide their attendees—all of them healthcare professionals—with the chance to hear from the heart of a victim who had been affected by one of their errors.

The week before the event, it occurred to me to ask him, "How many people usually attend one of these meetings?"

"It's hard to say, Ridley. Usually there are about thirty to forty doctors, nurses, and other staff. For something like this, I'm hoping to have twice as many . . . maybe eighty or so."

That morning, as I made my way to the podium in their auditorium, I was blown away to find out that there were almost 400 attendees in that room and in an overflow room the hospital had set up for the occasion. Wayne was just as surprised.

As I'd watched people filter into the room that morning,

I couldn't decide if they had come to learn some new insight ... or to see how the preacher from Middle Tennessee would lash out at their hospital.

I began with a slide show that Tonda had helped me piece together with pictures of my family, of the accident, and of Josh's days in the hospital. After the final notes of the background song faded, I stepped to the podium, shaking with nerves—and turned to face a crowd that was wiping away tears. Even some of the veteran physicians in the room had become emotional at the sights and sounds of Josh's story. After praying for weeks about how to address these people, I began my talk in the only place where I thought I could:

My name is Ridley Barron, and I am the proud father of the three children you see on the screen behind me. Over the past several months, I've been asked many times why I wanted to come and do this, and I can honestly tell you, I don't really want to be here. I'd rather be home chasing that little fellow, Josh, around the house. I also want to assure you today that I am not here to make you feel bad. In fact, I'm here first of all to tell you thank you.

Thank you for what you did. My son was brought into your hospital on April 9, after the car accident that you saw, and for five days your efforts kept him alive—to the point where he was improving. I want to thank you for what you do, because I know that quite often the job you do is a thankless one. It is glamorized by shows like *ER* [a hit TV series at the time] to be something it's really not. I also want to thank you for what you *will* do, because thousands of patients will come to this hospital this year and their story, fortunately, will not end like mine.

But the reason I am here is because I am more than a statistic. My son is more than just a number. If, by sharing our story, we can make you not just one of the best hospitals in America, but *the* best hospital in America, then I feel like my son's death is worth something.

There are a lot of things I want to say to you, and I promise you, none of them are bitter. I am not angry with you. I'm not angry with the pharmacist who made the mistake. I tried to make it very clear through Wayne and Bill and several others that when you deal with things like this, you are dealing with human beings . . . and mistakes sometimes get made. But on the other side of that, there's this realization that one time out of one, I came here and I lost a loved one. You see, I was never at your hospital before, and I've never been since. So your track record with me is not great.

I don't say that to belittle you. It's just to say that as an individual, I wish it could have been better. I don't understand everything that happened with my son. In fact, as I sat and listened to your very wonderful leaders and doctors here, I don't understand half of the things they said to you. I don't understand what took place that day with Josh. In fact, probably to understand the story a little bit better, you need to know what happened . . .

It was an amazing morning of healing for me. I think it was for the hospital staff as well. There were so many thoughts racing through my mind, I couldn't imagine that what I was saying made any sense. I cried twice—once to the point where I had to stop and regain my composure.

I wasn't the only one. God was making His end of the deal come true: Josh's death was counting for something. What happened to our family would be used to bring good and, more importantly, glory to God.

I concluded:

I don't know what you think when you see me. I don't know what you feel when you see me. I hope it's more than a statistic. I hope you see a real, live, walking, talking human being—a customer of yours. But my prayer, more than anything else, is that as you go from here today, you will understand that every detail you pay attention to is worth it. Every time you look at the chart a second or a third or fourth time, it is worth it. Even those times when you have to stay a little bit longer to make sure the details are taken care of, it's worth it.

I applaud the fact that you are one of the safest hospitals in America, but that makes no difference to me. It makes no difference to me because I can't take that home to my kids tonight. My prayer for you, for all the great things you do, is that more and more you won't have to say the kind of things I had to hear: "I'm sorry; your son is gone."

After we finished, I made my way up the aisle toward the rear of the auditorium. There were hospital officials who wanted to give their condolences. Person after person stopped to tell me thanks, to hug me, and to apologize on behalf of the hospital. About halfway to the back, I noticed a young lady in a pharmacist's coat. She was approaching me with tears in her eyes. A lump formed in my throat. Could this be the lady who had made the error? I wasn't sure, since to this point, the hospital had not allowed the pharmacist and me to talk.

The woman stepped forward and reached up to put her arms around my neck, her eyes swollen and red from crying. She introduced herself and began, "I work here in the pharmacy at the hospital." Then, as if reading my mind, she added quickly, "I'm not the one who made the mistake that day. But I am her friend. She asked me to come and apologize on her behalf today because she couldn't be here—she had a child at home with a personal need."

"Thank you," I uttered. I didn't know what else to say.

"Mr. Barron," the woman continued, "I know she would have loved to hear your talk this morning. She would love to know that you have forgiven her and that there is no bitterness there."

"You mean she's never heard that . . . ever?" My heart dropped. "That was one of the first things I asked the lawyers to do for me—to tell her I forgave her. Would you do me a favor?" She nodded her head anxiously. "I understand they have recorded this presentation today for others in the hospital to watch. Would you be sure that she gets a copy of that DVD?" The woman nodded again in affirmation. We hugged and she headed back up the stairs.

Upon exiting the auditorium, I followed Wayne to his office, where we shared a soft drink and talked casually about the kids and our move to Franklin. I was so relieved that God had done His part, and that good had come from Josh's senseless death. I truly believed that, despite my inadequate knowledge of health care or hospital practice, my talk that morning would bring some positive change. I was glad that it was over . . . or at least, I thought it was. But God wasn't finished yet. In fact, He was just beginning.

"Ridley," Wayne began. I loved that Wayne and I were now developing a friendship and were on a first-name basis. "I thought this morning was marvelous. You did a wonderful job. Better than we could have hoped. Now I have a question to ask you."

"Sure, Wayne. I'll be glad to do whatever I can."

"Would you do it again?" he ventured. "Would you be willing to share your story with others? I really believe that we could share it in a lot of different places and have a real impact. What do you think?"

I said yes without hesitation. I didn't have a clue what that would look like, and didn't realize that Wayne was dreaming of something bigger than a return visit to the hospital in Savannah. I didn't even think ahead to the prospect of me standing in front of people who represented a field I had no background in or knowledge of. I simply knew that this tragedy being used to make a difference would fulfill a dream of mine.

However, the more I thought about what I had just agreed to, the more skeptical I became. Would anyone really want to hear me—this average guy—share his story? Would these seasoned medical professionals be willing to let me into their meetings and conferences and, more importantly, would they be willing to hear the things I shared with them?

Before I experienced God's mind-blowing answer to these questions, He responded to one of my foremost concerns.

It had been only a few weeks since my trip to Savannah. I was rambling around in my kitchen, doing my best to try and stir up something for dinner, when the phone rang. I answered the call as I poured beans into a pot.

"Mr. Barron?" The voice at the other end sounded very timid.

"Yes, this is he."

"Mr. Barron, my name is _____." There was a long pause. "I am the pharmacist from Savannah. The one who made the error."

I can't recall all the emotions that hit me in those next few moments—surprise, fear, sadness, pain. I took a deep breath, and she and I shared our hearts for several minutes, as well as many tears. The woman apologized numerous times, and numerous times I assured her that she was forgiven, that there was no bitterness. I even encouraged her to go back to work. She said, "No, I'm enjoying being retired now. I just hate so terribly what happened. And . . ." another pause, "I just needed to know that you forgave me."

I said it again for her then . . . and I say it again now in case she is reading: "You are forgiven. I do not hold ill will toward you."

Let me tell you this. Bitterness is a poison that kills no one but the person who holds on to it. I had to let go of what had happened for the pharmacist's sake, the driver's sake— and for me.

That phone call was followed a week or so later by another one from Savannah. This time, it was Wayne Marchant calling to follow up on his invitation for me to speak again. "Are you sure you would be willing to do it all again?"

"Yes," I said, still thinking he simply wanted me back in Savannah. "I'd be glad to do whatever you believe will help."

"Great," he responded. "I have you scheduled to speak to an association of children's hospitals in Boston in October."

I think I screamed into the phone. "No, Wayne! I can't do that! I'm not qualified! Why would anyone want to listen to what I have to say? I don't know the language; I don't have the background . . ."

Wayne was well prepared for my response, almost as if he had known what I would say. "That's exactly why we need it, Ridley. We hear numbers from professionals in the medical field all the time. What we need is someone from the other side of the bed—the face of a victim."

I knew he was right. But that didn't calm my fears.

When I did ultimately get to Boston (in October 2005), that nagging feeling that I was out of place only increased. I was scheduled to speak to the National Association of Children's Hospitals and Related Institutions (NACHRI). Just the name alone made me feel way out of place. I spoke that day anyway, and shared many of the same thoughts that I had shared the previous December in Savannah. When it was all said and done, all I wanted to do was get on the plane and get home. I simply was drained from retelling Josh's story.

The opening of old emotional wounds had tired me out physically and mentally. But the NACHRI people were wonderful. I left that day with dozens of business cards from other interested hospital administrators, and my eyes were opened to the door that God had just walked me through. He was going to do something through this, I could tell. I just wasn't aware of how good it could be.

My brother-in-law, Keith, had made the journey with me to keep me company and encourage me. As we got on the plane, Keith was all excited. I remember him saying, "Rid, Wayne was right! Your story has tremendous potential for bringing change. You better get ready for this to take off!"

Me? I was just relieved to be off the stage and on my way home to Tennessee.

14

As December of 2004 rolled around, the kids and I were facing our first Christmas without Sarah Ellen and Josh. I had no idea what to expect, no expectations of what the holiday would hold. But when you lose someone, as I had, you note major dates and holidays to prepare yourself mentally and emotionally. You have to. When you are a parent of kids who have lost someone, you work even harder to prepare yourself.

But what you don't think about and really can't plan for are the "simple moments." That's the name I've given to those times during the course of ordinary days when you don't know why, but something causes you to grieve some more.

It happened to me a couple of times in Douglas before we moved. The first time was the day we ran out of flour. My mom had been fixing some lunch and needed a little flour. Sarah and I had talked about so many things and shared so many secrets with each other, including the major things we needed to know and the "what ifs." But she had never told me where she kept the extra flour. Now, any other day in any other circumstances, it would be no big deal: I would have either found the flour or gone to the store and bought some more. On this day, out of frustration, I lashed out at Mom and then disappeared for a while just to cry. I needed Sarah.

The second time came one day when I went to our mailbox. At the foot of the mailbox post was a small flower bed that Sarah and I had put in. Every spring, she and I would go to the local nursery, purchase a few white and pink begonias (favorites of hers), and plant them. That day, I walked to the mailbox and, as I got closer, I realized for the first time that there were no begonias—Sarah wasn't there to plant them. My heart sank and I began to cry.

Those simple moments have an ability to come unannounced. They lurk behind an empty pantry, unpaid bills, unreturned phone calls, or a song on the radio. There is simply no way you can prepare yourself for them all. So you handle each one as it comes, in its own time.

Just the month before, in November, I'd had another first: my first date since becoming single again.

I was a nervous wreck. I hated dating. I really didn't even like it in high school and college; now, as a thirty-seven-year-old father of two, I was almost squeamish about the prospect. In fact, I never would have dated again, nor been ready to, if it hadn't been for conversations that Sarah Ellen and I had in the months before she died. During those conversations we talked about the "what ifs" that go along with a spouse's death. I had assured her that, if something were to happen to me, I would want her to try to find someone else—to find happiness again, as well as someone to help her raise our kids. She had assured me of the same, even going so far as to jokingly threaten to come back and haunt me if I didn't.

Yet dating was such a chore for me. Frankly, the dating game at my age was loaded with plenty of strange people. Many of the ladies I met were looking for a pastor because they somehow believed that I could fix the problems that filled their life. Others saw me as a welcome respite from the issues that had accompanied their previous marriages. Even with all of that, though, I was very fortunate. The women I dated were—for the most part—amazing, godly women with wonderful characteristics. Most of them loved my kids, and my kids returned that love for the ones who hung around.

Ultimately, in these relationships, I had to follow my heart. That in itself was a scary proposition, because I knew the state of my heart: I loved Sarah Ellen. I still do. There was not one moment of my life with her that I would have traded. Yes, there were some difficult times. But Sarah was an incredible woman, a beautiful wife, and a very precious mother. Those traits are hard to find, and even harder for someone else to have to follow behind.

There's no question that I doubted myself, especially after those first few dating relationships. With each one that didn't work out, I wondered if there would be another chance. And with each one that didn't work out, my heart was growing more tired. I got to the point that I only wanted to love my children and focus my energies on them and the church. I convinced myself that maybe that was what God wanted too.

Still, there were blind dates arranged by loving friends and meetings that led to dates. I was introduced to one young lady by a church friend; another I met when taking my kids to the dentist's office. Most of them were women I was blessed to meet. But in between, there were matches that weren't ideal. One lady I chatted with was very sweet. We had talked about what we both did for a career, what our hobbies were, and what we wanted to find in another person. Then, she promptly asked me to leave my kids home one night and come over and sleep with her. I just about fell on the floor. I emailed her back and said, "Thanks . . . I think. But do you remember what I do for a living? Do you remember Who I work for?" Needless to say, that relationship came to a screeching halt. Almost as fast as the conversation I had with a wonderful lady from the Midwest a few weeks later.

She and I began talking after we met on one of those online dating services. Believe me, this time I made it perfectly clear that I was a pastor. Things were going great. She was very pretty, very down-to-earth. She enjoyed sports, kids, going to church . . . I really thought this one had tremendous potential—until the day she popped the question. Not THAT question. She simply asked, "What kind of church do you pastor?"

"I'm part of a Southern Baptist church. It's not like most Southern Baptist churches, but we are affiliated with the denomination and cooperate in working with them."

The other end of the phone was dead silent. Then, in a sudden burst, she said, "Well, I guess we're done then. I can't date you, so there is probably no point in even continuing to talk."

I was speechless. What had just happened? Did I miss something? Then she explained, "I'm from the Church of Jesus Christ of Latter-Day Saints." In other words, a Mormon. "If you and I dated, you would probably tell me that my church has Jesus all wrong. You'd probably tell me I need to look at the Bible again and rethink what I believe. Your theology is different from mine."

All I could think to say was, "Probably. But didn't you just do the same to me?" End of relationship.

Looking back, I can see how each situation was preparing me for what God was getting ready to do in that area of my life. In the meantime, though, my heart was growing wearier. Even the good relationships and conversations drained me emotionally. I just wasn't sure that there was another wife in my future—or a stepmother for my kids. But I would have to trust that God would take care of us, no matter what.

15

One early December morning, a dear friend of mine called and began to chat with me about the church and how the family was doing. About halfway into our conversation, he asked, "Ridley, how would you feel about someone doing an article on you and the kids and the church plant?"

My heart kind of skipped a beat. This would be just another way that God could use the tragedy in our family for something good. While our church had yet to launch, we were fast approaching our January start date. Maybe this would serve as a boost to that event as well.

"Of course," I said. "It would be some great publicity for the church, and I'm sure the kids would enjoy the opportunity. How do we go about doing that?"

"Leave that to me," he replied. "I've got a contact with the newspaper, and we'll see where it goes from there."

Just a few days later, I received a phone call from a religion writer with *The Tennessean*—Nashville's largest newspaper. She set up an appointment to come by the house, ask a few questions, and take some pictures. She seemed really interested in hearing about every aspect of what our family had been through.

After finishing our time together, she thanked me and said, "This will probably be on the front page of the religion section the first Friday in January." In my mind, the timing—only a few weeks away—would be perfect: the Friday before our church's first public worship time together.

Boy, did I underestimate what God would do! Friday, January 7 rolled in cool and crisp. It was going to be a busy weekend as the team and I prepared for our first service project on Saturday morning and our church launch on Sunday. I got the kids up and sent them off to school without mentioning that it was the day that the article was to be published. I knew there was still a chance that it wouldn't even make the editor's cut. Still, on the way to the office, I grabbed a paper at the convenience store. Sure enough, there was no article.

A couple of hours later I was headed to downtown Nashville for a lunch appointment with a friend. My cell phone rang, and the caller ID showed a number I did not recognize. When I answered, I recognized the voice of the reporter from *The Tennessean*.

"Mr. Barron," she began, "I hope you're doing well today. I intended to call you earlier this week and simply got sidetracked.

"I wanted to apologize to you," she said. When she hesitated, I took the opportunity to reassure her.

"Listen, you don't have to apologize to me. I understand how newspapers work. I knew that it would be a long shot for the article to make the paper. It's really not a big deal. I just appreciate you taking the time to come out and take pictures of the kids and all that."

She laughed. "Oh no, Mr. Barron. I wasn't apologizing because the article wasn't in the paper today. I was apologizing because I didn't let you know my news sooner. You see, when the editors read the article and saw your story, they wanted to move it from today's religion section to the front page of tomorrow's paper." She paused. "Mr. Barron, your article is going to be on the front page of the Saturday *Tennessean.*"

I was blown away. Once again, I was seeing God do what only God could do. Only a few months before, I had asked Him to bring good from the tragedy that had touched my life. Now, yet again, He was opening doors for my family's story to bring Him glory and help minister to others.

As the reporter had promised, the Saturday paper featured a large picture of Abby, Harrison, and me. The article was wonderfully done. It told a little about our church and about why the kids and I were back in Middle Tennessee. Then the writer turned her attention to the events surrounding the accident. I was very pleased about the tasteful way that she dealt with both subjects, and I called her to say thanks for handling everything so well. Of course, the kids were thrilled about having their picture in the paper.

It wasn't long after the article appeared that the phone calls began to come in, along with emails and a few hand-written notes. The response was truly overwhelming. Word came from moms and dads, sisters and brothers, people who were recovering from loss, and some who were in the middle of their own personal trials. Some people were just looking for a person to talk to. Others were seeking a little peace. Most wanted to know about my personal journey and my relationship with Christ. They wanted to know how God had carried me through the hurt and pain of losing Sarah and Josh.

The response was so great that one of the leaders in my church came and asked if I would need some part-time help to respond to all the messages and inquiries. My simple answer was no; I couldn't do that. I knew that these people had reached out to me and, as long as I was able to manage it, I wanted to be the one to reply.

I can't tell you how amazed I was. It wasn't so much that there was a response; I expected that there might be a few folks who would want to send their sympathies or share their stories. But the volume of responses was mind-boggling. Within a few weeks I had communicated with people from forty-eight states and three countries. Thinking back now, I live with a regret that maybe I didn't get to deal with every person in as personal a way as I would have loved to. However, all the comments helped me to think specifically about the emotions I had felt and the challenges

I had faced. Putting what I had been through into words for others helped me to process all that had been happening and was continuing to happen in my heart.

The Saturday morning the article was released, Ridgeview Church was on the sidewalk at a local grocery store, handing out free hot chocolate and water to customers in an effort to let them know about our church's first service the following day. I was pleased to meet folks of all ages who had seen the article. Many took the time to share how cool it was to hear how God had provided for our family.

The next day was D-day—the launch of Ridgeview Community Church was finally on us. What an incredible day it was! More than 300 people showed up at the school where we met to help us start this amazing journey. It all seemed so surreal. I remember thinking that morning how weird it was to be greeting people without Sarah Ellen by my side. She had been such a huge part of everything I did. She was my best friend, my ministry partner, my first lady . . . and now she was gone.

Though that first Sunday went very well, it was tainted by the memories of Sarah that lingered in my mind. If Sarah had been there, she would have served gracefully as the pastor's wife. She made people feel so at ease and was careful to include others. She was warm and welcoming and had truly been a gifted partner in ministry for me over the twelve years of our marriage. It was hard to believe we weren't doing this together.

As time went on, the church grew—much slower than I wanted, but grew nonetheless. I was coaching baseball, and I even coached Abby's soccer team for a couple of seasons despite having no clue about soccer. The speaking opportunities continued to increase too. I was flying to places I'd never been, being introduced to fascinating people. At an event at Duke University, I met a wonderful professor from Florida State University. She and I shared a Coke while she talked about the importance of what I was doing and how I could make it a much stronger presentation.

In Jacksonville, Florida, at Wolfson Children's Hospital, I had the pleasure of speaking with Scott Waddle, a Navy officer who asked permission to promote my message wherever he went to speak. He, too, was familiar with tragedy as the former commanding officer of the USS *Greenville*, a submarine that had surfaced off the coast of Hawaii in 2001 and accidentally sunk a Japanese fishing trawler. The accident had killed several Japanese students and gained international attention. I was humbled to be speaking with this man and astounded at his own humility about that event and his life.

Probably one of the most incredible people I met along the way was Dr. Fay Rozovsky. Fay is a consultant. She invited me to Boston for a speaking engagement in 2006 where we shared the podium and then had the opportunity to discuss ideas over Starbucks. Fay represents the kind of person who is making a huge difference in health care in America. She is a sweet little Jewish fireball with deep passion and a wealth of knowledge. I count her as one of the many treasures that God has brought to me along this journey.

Since that first day together in 2006, Fay and I have shared the stage a couple more times and passed a few ideas back and forth. She has recommended a book or two as well. She even planted trees in Israel in honor of my family. I hope she gets to read this book someday so she'll understand how much her friendship has meant to me.

As 2006 came to a close, the pieces of my life were falling into place. Ridgeview Church, despite its ups and downs, was seeing the vision that we had cast for her and beginning to take shape. God was working through my speaking engagements and positioning me in places so that I could feel His grace in incredible ways. But my personal journey and growth seemed stalled. I couldn't quite put my finger on what it was or why I felt that way. Maybe I had simply settled into a rut.

That Christmas was the third since Sarah's death, and it was probably the most prepared I had felt for the holiday since the day of the accident. The kids and I decorated the house with the help of a friend. We worked hard to make things really nice and create that holiday feeling. But Christmas Day itself took me by surprise.

It began like usual, with Harrison and Abby rolling out of bed prepared to eat some breakfast and then rip into presents. But somewhere along the way, feelings shifted. Harrison and I had a disagreement about something, so I asked him to come into my room and talk with me for just a bit.

"What's wrong today? It's supposed to be one of the best days of the year," I chided. "You're supposed to be happy and excited about your gifts and hanging out with your cousins later today. What's up?"

He began to cry. "I miss Mom."

I have no idea where that came from. His honesty caught me by surprise—almost as much as my own did: "I do too, buddy. I do too."

The next thing I knew, Harrison crawled into the bed next to me and began to cry harder. He rolled up close to me, and for the next hour, we remembered Mom. We talked about her Christmas breakfast casserole she made every year, and how he missed her being at home when he came in from school. We laughed at the funny dance she used to do for him and Abby. We cried. We laughed. We were silent. And then . . . we were done.

To this day, I don't know what Abby did while we shared that moment. I like to believe that God kept her entertained while Harrison and I went through one more stage of our healing.

16

One evening in February 2007, I was lying on the couch watching a ballgame while Harrison and Abby entertained themselves nearby. It was really one of those nights when I was content just to be there with the kids. I didn't want to talk to anyone, and I didn't want to be with anyone. But then the phone rang. I checked the caller ID. It was my brother-in-law, Keith. I've been blessed with some of the best in-laws in the world. Keith is no exception. Otherwise, I might have let voicemail handle it.

Still, I am sure I sounded less than thrilled when I answered.

"Hey, Rid. It's Keith. Tonda and I are over here at the cooking school for a class. We just met somebody that I think you'd like to meet. Are you interested?"

I have to admit that I was curious. Keith and Tonda had respectfully stayed out of my dating life to that point unless I asked their opinion. So this recommendation stirred my heart a little. But I was also tired. Tired of dating. Tired of the games. Tired of getting my hopes up. I even wondered sometimes if I was ready to be back in the dating scene. So I said, "Nope."

I think my answer surprised even me. But then I caught myself, realizing how callous that must have sounded, so I added, "Who is she?"

"Well, she's a very attractive young lady. Got two girls from previous marriages." *Uh-oh*, I thought. *May be some baggage I'm not up to dealing with.* Keith continued, "Her name is Lisa DeHart."

Lightbulb! "The realtor? Isn't she the chick whose picture is on the grocery carts?"

"Yeah, that's her. She's really nice, and I think she might be interested in going out. What do you say?"

"I don't know. Let me think about it."

"Alright. Call me tomorrow, and we'll talk."

I hung up the phone and tried to get back into the game on TV. I had seen Lisa's picture numerous times and thought to myself that she was a strikingly attractive woman. But beyond that, what did I know about her? *A blind date*, I thought to myself. *Do I really want to go on another setup like that?*

It turned out that Lisa had been at the cooking school with a friend of hers—Jo—and her husband. Jo had told Lisa about me three years before, after meeting Harrison at the school where she taught. When she heard our story and all that we had been through, Jo asked Lisa to pray for my kids and me. So Lisa did. For three years.

Lisa actually lived just around the corner from me, though I didn't know it then. Several times a week she would pass by my house on her way to work or while she was out running. Each time she did, she would pray.

That night, while sitting at the table at the cooking school, Tonda began to explain to Jo and Lisa why they had moved to the area. As soon as Jo recognized the story, she nudged Lisa and said, "This is him—the guy I was telling you about . . . the one you've been praying for. This is the guy I've been wanting to introduce you to."

As Keith relayed the story to me the next day, I was a little excited to hear how the connection was made. Still, the thought of another blind date made me apprehensive—something that Keith was apparently picking up on. So he offered to make it a triple date with him and Tonda, Jo and her husband, and Lisa and me. I relented, and we planned on the coming Friday. My stomach was in knots.

For the rest of the week, I tried to ignore this looming event, distracting myself with meeting after meeting and other activities. Yet, there was no way around the fact that I had opened myself up to another date.

By the time Friday arrived, my enthusiasm for the evening had reached a new low. I greeted my babysitter that night with a bit of disappointment, having hoped that she would call and cancel at the last minute. I kissed Harrison and Abby good night and hopped into my Avalanche. I don't know why I was feeling so desperate about this particular date; I knew this was what it would take if I was ever going to find someone else to spend my life with. Nevertheless, about halfway to the restaurant where the six of us had planned to meet, I took my cell phone out of my pocket and dialed my sister's number. Everything in me wanted to call her and tell her I wouldn't make it tonight because I wasn't feeling well. It wasn't a lie, I reasoned, because I really wasn't feeling good about the date. Yet instead of pressing "send," I clicked "end" and put the phone away. It wasn't the right thing to do. How would it make Lisa feel? How would I feel if I were in her shoes?

I eased the Avalanche into the parking lot at the restaurant. Glancing at the entrance, I noticed a group standing inside the doorway. I killed the engine, took a deep sigh, and muttered to no one in particular, "Well, here goes nothing." Then, realizing that there was only one other Person who could hear me, I threw a quick prayer in His direction: "God, You know I'm not real excited about this, so can You just get me through the evening?" How's that for a positive expectation?

As I walked toward the front door, I had this crazy feeling that the whole world was just on the other side of the large, tinted windows, watching to see how this thing would go. Opening the door, I stepped into a small circle that included Jo, her husband, and Lisa. *Just my luck*, I thought to myself. *I got here before Keith and Tonda, and now I have to pretend to enjoy this conversation until they get here.*

Keith and Tonda arrived a few minutes later, but it would be a lie to say that the dinner went better. Because of the real-estate connection between Lisa, Jo (also a realtor), and Keith (a title lawyer at the time), the bulk of the conversation centered around their work and the cooking school class they had all enjoyed together. For that ninety minutes or so over dinner, from my corner seat at our restaurant table, I watched a ballgame on the TV that was just over Lisa's shoulder. Every now and then I would be thrown a morsel of conversation, but nothing more than that.

As the wait staff was removing our plates, I was thinking I was off the hook—the evening was over and I could head home. But then Tonda spoke up, "Our house is just around the corner from here. Why don't we all go back over there and enjoy some dessert? Keith made some fabulous stuff in the kitchen today."

Dang, I thought. *I had just about made it, free and clear. Why did she have to bring that up? Now I'm obligated to go over to their house.*

We exited the restaurant and were gripped by the cold night air—February in Middle Tennessee was in full force. I pulled my jacket up around my chin and started toward my truck. Out of the corner of my eye I could see Lisa standing on the sidewalk. She looked almost lost, waiting for some kind of clue as to whom she should be riding with. Keith and Tonda were halfway to their car, and Jo and Chris had already made it to theirs.

Not wanting to look like I had no manners, I turned back toward Lisa and half-heartedly asked, "You want to ride with me?"

Her answer was equally half-hearted. She had to be thinking to herself, *What's the other option? Walking four miles?*

I escorted her to the passenger side of the truck and allowed her to slide in before shutting the door. By the time we reached the first stoplight a few hundred yards away, we were laboring to have a conversation. I could feel the awkwardness in the few words we shared and in the telling silence in between, so I did the only thing I knew to do: I got brazenly honest with her. What did I have to lose?

"Look," I said, "I don't like dating. Never have. Not in high school or in college. But I really loved being married and I'd love to be married again. If it were up to me, God would just put a lightbulb over the head of the girl He would like for me to marry, and we could skip this whole dating thing. I wouldn't have to play the games or sort through the people who just weren't right for me. I don't know if that makes sense or not, but I just don't like dating."

I realized I had a death grip on the steering wheel. I glanced toward Lisa. In the glow of the dashboard light, I couldn't tell if she was sad or mad or just deep in thought about what I had shared. I expected Lisa to say something like, "Stop the truck or take me home." Instead, she responded in a completely unexpected way. Though she was silent, the passing streetlights revealed a smile on her face. *Okay,* I thought, *she is either alright with what I shared or she is thinking to herself that I am a real nut case.*

It was then that something incredible happened. It was like a switch flipped on, and the whole evening turned into something completely different.

It turns out we had a great time at my sister's house. The conversation was much lighter, much more enjoyable. We laughed and joked and shared more about ourselves. Lisa clued me in a little more about her family and her girls. We talked about our pasts and spoke of some of the struggles of raising kids all alone. It was easy to see that we had much in common.

Finally, it was time to head home. It was only then that I learned that Lisa lived less than a mile from my house. This time, I jumped at the chance to give her a ride.

It was after eleven when we pulled into her driveway. I shut off the truck and walked around to open her door. The temperature was fast approaching single digits and the wind was unforgiving. When we reached the front door of her house, she unlocked it and then immediately stepped between the open door and me as if to say, "You're not coming into my home."

I couldn't tell what her angle was, but the entire second half of the evening had been a huge success as far as I was concerned. So I asked to come in anyway.

She sighed and said, "Sure. Just for a second." Then she

stepped back and allowed me just enough room to get inside the doorway and shut the door. I got the feeling that this was as far as I was going. The small talk had come to an end.

"I had a nice evening, Lisa. Thanks for taking the time to go out. I'd like to do it again if you're interested."

She nodded.

"Can I get your number?"

As Lisa slipped into her office to grab a business card on which to write down her cell number, I glanced around at what I could see of her house. *Very nice*, I thought to myself. *It's clean. Nicely decorated. Not too crazy.*

Her footsteps brought my focus back to her. "Here you go," she said as she slipped the card into my hand. She continued past me to the front door and put her hand on the knob.

It was clear what she was trying to communicate. She'd had a good time, but opening her door to me was not the same thing as opening her heart to me.

Still, I took a chance. "Lisa, before I go . . . do you mind if I pray with you?"

She stopped in her tracks and turned to face me, hesitating only a second before mumbling, "Yes, I'd like that." She walked the three steps from the door back to my side and laid her head on my shoulder. As I prayed, she began to cry. The soft sound of her crying was muffled by my jacket, but the tears falling down her face betrayed what was going on.

My only thought was, *Oh no! What have I done wrong now?*

Once I finished, Lisa pulled away and looked at me with these incredible blue eyes that I really hadn't noticed until then. She began to explain, "I hope you don't think I'm crazy, but for years I've wanted a man to come into my home and be a spiritual leader for me and my girls. I've never had that till this very moment . . . even if it is only temporary. Thank you." Then she stepped toward the door once more, opened it, and said, "Thank you again."

I told her I'd give her a call soon and floated to the car. The brutal February wind made little difference to me now. I was feeling very warm inside.

17

I called Lisa the next night. She was at a Predators game—
Nashville's hockey team—with her dad, so we only talked
briefly. Before we hung up though, we made plans for our
next date: Valentine's Day.

The days are really short in Middle Tennessee in February, so by the time I started over to Lisa's house with Harrison and Abby in tow, the sun was already sinking below
the horizon. Lisa and I had agreed to let her oldest daughter
keep the kids while we went out. Putting our kids together
so early was something I would never have done before, but
for some reason, it just seemed to make sense this time.

Since it was just our second date, I had decided that I
wouldn't put any pressure on her by buying some sappy card
or meaningless gift. After all, I still didn't know much about
her. So I reasoned it would be better just to enjoy this night.

Lisa, however, opened the front door with a gift in her
hand.

So much for your reasoning, Romeo, I said to myself. If I
could have kicked myself, I would've found a way to do it as
we walked into her den.

She and I introduced the kids to one another. In addition to her fifteen-year-old daughter, Lisa had an eight-year-old girl. The four kids promptly disappeared upstairs to the bonus room to begin their evening, while I sat down in the kitchen to open the present Lisa had for me.

Slipping the ribbon off of the shirt box, I explained why I hadn't taken the time to get her anything. The top slipped off easily to reveal dozens of Treasure Chocolate candies. Lisa had remembered my confession from the first night that I was a major chocoholic. Written inside the lid was this verse:

For where your treasure is, there your heart will be also.
Matthew 6:21

Pretty cute.

In the middle of the box, taped in among all of the chocolate, was a lightbulb. A 100-watt lightbulb. *Okay,* I thought. *That's sweet. But what in the world is it all about?* Then it hit me. She hadn't just remembered my affinity for chocolate; she had remembered my comment from the truck, " . . . If I had my way, God would just put a lightbulb over the head of the woman I should marry."

Lisa was auditioning! I almost fell off the barstool.

I didn't know how to respond. Should I run? Should I act ignorant? I chose to be a man and see where this would lead. I can't honestly tell you that I did it without a little bit of fear, though.

As Lisa and I dated over the next several weeks, we would alternate between time alone and time with the kids, knowing that if this relationship was going anywhere, it would affect all six of us. She and I both were blown away by how well our kids got along. They played together, went swimming together, even treated each other with respect. I was very pleasantly surprised.

Lisa and I seemed to be hitting on all cylinders as well. We would spend our time over dinner talking about really important things: how we were raising our kids, expectations for a future spouse, our beliefs regarding God and the church, how we handled conflict. It seemed on the surface as if everything was just right.

Yet underlying the great dates and the memories we were creating was this gnawing memory of a statement I had made just a few months after Sarah died. I had been talking with a friend of mine about the future and what that might look like and about dating again. Finally, she asked the question that many people—including me—had been wondering: "Would you ever date a divorced woman?"

I wasn't sure how to respond. Was she asking because she had someone particular in mind, or because she genuinely wanted to know? I chose to believe the latter and answered with what was on my heart: "No, I probably wouldn't. The divorced people I know tend to have baggage and emotional snares. I just don't think I want to go through that."

Now, three and a half years later, those words echoed in my mind every time I was with Lisa. And for that reason, I simply would not tell her I loved her. I told her I had fun with her; I told her I thought she was amazing; I told her that I wanted to see her again. I just could not bring myself to say those three critical words until I could be sure they were right.

One day at lunch, it all came to a head. Lisa had invited me to come from the church office to her house, where she was going to fix us a quiet lunch. The thought was kind . . . but I knew something was up. When we finished lunch, I moved from the barstool to a chair in the corner of the kitchen. As I settled into the seat, Lisa followed me. She then pulled around a chair from the table, plopped down in front of me, and looked me in the eye.

"I need to talk to you," she said. I had never seen Lisa this serious. I was a little scared. But I also was thinking, *Man, I could look into those blue eyes for a really long time.*

She continued, "I want to have a minute to let you know something. It's very important that you hear what I am about to say. I have told you several times that I love you. I do love you—but I don't want you to think that when I tell you that, I'm pressuring you to say the same. I do want to hear those words from you someday, but only when you are ready."

I hesitated for just a second. She had opened a door that we needed to go through. I felt this time was as good as any. "I guess I need to tell you something as well," I replied. "I made a commitment a long time ago that I would never say those words to any woman until I knew it was right. I believe those words are overused and abused in our culture. Honestly, there is a lot of soul-searching that I need to do before I think I'll be ready for that to happen."

Her eyes told me she wanted more, so I added, "Just pray for me, because when that time is right, I believe God will let me know it."

I came away from that lunch more than just a little relieved that we had at least crossed that bridge. But I knew that the soul-searching had to take place and that, to be fair to Lisa and both sets of kids, I needed to come to some peace with all of these questions before we went much further.

One March Saturday, about six weeks into our relationship, Lisa came by the house. It was a gorgeous day, with abundant sunshine and temperatures that were perfect for being outside. Lisa pulled up in her little red convertible. She had a big, beautiful smile on her face, and she looked amazing sitting there in the sun. The timing could not have been worse for this conversation.

"You want to go for a ride on the Trace?" I asked.

"Sure," she replied. "It's a great day for it."

The Trace is the Natchez Trace—a 444-mile parkway that

follows an old trail that early settlers used to take between Nashville and lower Mississippi. Today, it's a national parkway that winds through beautiful scenery, and it's a favorite spot for Sunday-afternoon drivers and avid bikers.

Lisa and I drove onto the Trace and rode for a while, and then pulled into one of the many parking areas that dot the trail. Lisa's look told me she was very curious.

"I thought we were going to ride. What are you doing?" she asked.

"We need to talk. I wanted to get away from the kids and come to a place where we would not be interrupted."

"Okay," she said. "What are we talking about?"

"We need to take a break," I blurted. Her face sank, the glow draining quickly from her eyes. "Remember me saying that there was some soul-searching I needed to do? I think it's really important that I do that before we go any further in this relationship. It wouldn't be fair to you or me to get too wrapped up in this thing without being more confident of where I'm going."

The minute I said *thing*, I thought to myself, *You could have picked a better word.*

"A break? What do you mean by a break?" she asked. " . . . And for how long?"

Lisa's face was no longer turned toward me. She was looking back through the front windshield, and her gaze was way off in the distance. This news was not sitting well.

"I don't know, honestly. It could be a week or a month or

forever. I just don't know. But you and I both believe . . . we both want this thing to be God's will. That's all I want is to just make sure it's God's will."

I paused briefly and then, feeling pretty certain about what she was thinking, I tried to reassure her: "This isn't because of anything you have done wrong or anything you should have done better."

The tears in her eyes confirmed that I wasn't doing a very good job. Heck, I wasn't even sure that I believed what I was saying. Lisa was looking at me again now, very intently. Her look told me she wanted more explanation. I didn't have any for her.

Needless to say, the drive back to my house was a quick one. When we got there, she hustled to say good-bye and head home. I walked into my house very numb and confused. I knew with all my heart that this was what I needed to do. I also knew that God had a plan. I just wasn't confident that my heart was in the place it needed to be for me to see that plan.

Immediately I set to work looking for answers. Every conversation, every time of solitude, every journal entry and search through the Bible was prayed about. I was talking with divorced people, reading blogs, poring over commentaries in my library, and talking with mentors. The way I saw it, there were two critical questions. First, what was God's perspective on Lisa's two failed marriages? Lisa's situation had been a clear example of a confused woman who had sought satisfaction in men. Her first marriage—before she became a Christ follower—had ended after the teenage dreams of a perfect relationship had given way to real life. Her second marriage—during which she was finally introduced to Christ—came crashing down due to lies, deceit, and infidelity, though she had stayed in the marriage for twelve years in an attempt to save it.

It was Lisa who had been cheated on, but I also knew what a lot of preachers preach about divorce, and I knew that preachers sometimes get it wrong out of their own prejudice. Yet there was a danger that I could do the same thing if I allowed my affections for Lisa to get in the way of the biblical answers I was seeking.

The second question on my mind—once the first question had been satisfactorily answered—was this: What was God's plan for the two of us? If He wanted us to continue dating—even just for a little while—was Lisa's baggage too much for me to deal with or expose my kids to? To be fair, was my own baggage too much for a woman and her daughters who had been through so much hell of their own?

None of these questions seemed easy. I settled in for a long process, figuring it would take a while to get to the bottom of these things. I was amazed at how quickly, clearly, and personally God spoke to me over the next few *days*.

18

The first "voice" to speak into my dilemma was a new friend. Ridgeview planted daughter churches early and often, and Mike served as the founding pastor of one that we established in the Nashville area. As fate would have it, he had done a paper on this very subject of divorce for some of his seminary work, and he let me read it only hours after my conversation with Lisa. It was an amazing paper—thorough in its search of Scripture and its analysis of the Bible's teaching versus prevailing thought. What struck me most as I read his work was a comparison of the Old Testament law to New Testament grace. The Old Testament law set up standards for living that were meant to define people's lives in relationship to God. New Testament grace came along to show us how far God's love would go to restore those who had missed the standard. I knew Lisa wasn't the only one who had fallen short of God's standard; I had as well, just perhaps in different ways. It comes with the territory of being human.

Two days later, another friend of mine talked to me about the oft-repeated verse from Malachi: "'I hate divorce,' says the LORD God of Israel, 'and I hate a man's covering himself with violence as well as with his garment,' says the LORD Almighty" (Malachi 2:16). I had heard this passage repeated so many times, and heard it preached by people I knew and respected. But that day my friend pointed out something to me that no one had mentioned before.

"Read the first three words again, Ridley." I did. "What do they say?"

"It says that God hates divorce. You can't get more obvious than that."

He nodded his head. "What does it *not* say?"

I was confused about what he was looking for, so I shrugged. He smiled and continued, "It says God hates *divorce* . . . not divorced people. God hates *divorce*. And who doesn't, Ridley? Ask anyone who has gone through the breakup of their marriage. You won't find one person who says that divorce was good for them, or that they were glad they went through it or had to drag their kids into it. God is saying He hates divorce because of what it does to individuals and to families. But He doesn't hate divorced people. There is grace for them, just as there is for the liar, the cheater, the overeater, the murderer. God wants to forgive their wrong and ease their pain."

Things were starting to get a little clearer now.

Another conversation was with a mentor of mine in the ministry as we shared lunch the next day. I told him about the previous conversations, as well as the results of my

Internet search of respected pastors' and writers' thoughts on the subject. Jerry summed up what I was feeling with these words: "Well, that will confuse the snot out of you. If you ask a hundred different theologians for their thoughts on divorce, you will get a hundred and one opinions."

I got his point. It was becoming increasingly clear that I would have to come to peace with this issue by prayerfully searching my own heart after reading the Bible.

I continued to dig. And what I found in Scripture was this amazing story of grace. Over and over again, I saw a God who desperately loves His creation. Because of His justice, He cannot ignore or turn His back on our sin. Yet because of His love, He devised a plan that gives every sinner (that's all of us) a second chance to get things right.

Given Lisa's painful past, she needed grace more than ever. Yet here is the amazing thing: as Lisa was picking up the pieces of her broken heart and giving them to Jesus in the years before we met, I was doing the same thing in a recliner in South Georgia. Her marriage had been ripped apart by selfishness and betrayal. Mine had been ripped apart by tragedy and death. Both of us needed strength and grace to move on. Both of us found it in our first love: Jesus Christ. That's what I consider a true twist of faith.

The end to my soul-searching came over breakfast with another trusted friend. It was Wednesday, just four days after my Saturday conversation with Lisa on the Natchez Trace. Roland has always been a trusted adviser and true friend—the kind who would shoot straight with me and be sure I had considered all angles. I don't know if he meant for things to unfold the way they did, but I believe with all my heart that God did.

Roland and I had both just finished the last bites of our omelettes. We were tucked away in a booth at the back of a diner where we often met to talk. As the conversation turned to Lisa's and my dating relationship and the journey that God had put me on, Roland ventured, "Let me ask you a question, Ridley. You're a pastor. You've got this young church in a growing community filled with people you are trying to reach. You start dating a woman who has been divorced—not once, but twice. Now you're thinking seriously about making it more serious. *Is this the kind of message you want to send to our community?*"

That question thundered loudly in my heart, and I felt as if God was saying, "Ridley, are you listening to what he is asking you? Are you prepared to hear what I really want to say to you? Is this the kind of message you want to send—I want to send—to this community?"

"Yes," I answered. "Absolutely, Roland. This is *exactly* the message that this community needs to hear. The church today is known more for what we are against than what we are for. It is time that people were reminded that we serve a very holy God who has lots of love and grace to give. They need to know that no one can run so far that God's grace can't find them.

"Lisa was forgiven the day she chose to follow Christ. So were you and I. Our community needs to know that the same grace is waiting for them regardless of their circumstances."

Roland simply nodded his head. "I think you know what you need to do, then."

And I did. I absolutely did.

I couldn't wait to get home from the office that day.

I couldn't wait to pick up the phone and call Lisa and tell her I needed to come over.

I couldn't wait to look into those eyes and let her know that my questions were answered and that I now had the freedom from God to move forward with wherever the relationship would take us.

I couldn't wait . . . so I didn't. I called her when I left the restaurant and told her everything that God had shown me.

We went out that night for dinner. Our conversation that evening opened the door for our relationship to move forward, unencumbered by the weight of doubt and fear. I felt like we were free to explore every possibility that God had for us. It was an amazing feeling. And Lisa's smile that evening told me she felt the same way.

19

Ridgeview Community Church continued to grow, and so did my kids. I could not believe how quickly time was passing. Harrison was now twelve years old and in middle school. He was playing baseball year 'round and fighting me hard on video games and computer time.

Abby had just turned nine a few months before. She continued to play soccer and make friends and have sleepovers.

They were busy but amazing days.

I prayed daily for both of my kids. I wasn't always sure of what they were feeling, but we talked as frequently as I could get them to open up. Those conversations seemed to reveal that they were adjusting to all of the changes and adapting to the void caused by Sarah Ellen's death. But Abby concerned me because she was fast approaching that age where little girls need their moms. I had gotten pretty good at ponytails and matching clothes, even for a color-blind guy. But I knew it would not be long before puberty and boys and pierced ears would show up on her radar, and I wasn't sure how well I could help her through those experiences.

My sister Tonda, along with several ladies at our church,

had been a huge help in dealing with the early stages of these challenges. The possibility of Lisa in our life gave me hope that, should things work out, Abby might have that godly female influence in her life every day—the kind I had been praying for so fervently.

Lisa and I continued to date, and I continued to pray about all areas of our relationship—the future, the relationships between our children, and the advice we were receiving from others who knew us. As she and I shared time together and talked about the future, it was apparent that God had His hand in things. I had learned quickly that dating the second time around is different. Many of the dating games that you get caught up in as a teen or young adult—the facades, the mental ploys, the posturing—are vastly diminished. Having found in Sarah a woman who was exactly what I had dreamed of and hoped for, it was much easier the second time around to be sure of the qualities I was seeking in the women I dated. I was constantly seeing those traits in Lisa, and while I knew that I would never find anyone just like Sarah, my heart was being drawn to all the similarities and values that drew Lisa and me together.

Our kids began to ask questions about marriage and becoming a family and our intentions for the future. I did my best to answer them honestly without leading them on or getting their hopes up. I knew they were excited about the possibility of having another mom, but I also knew that it would be a big mistake to let them believe there was potential there without knowing that for myself.

Finally, by mid-May, just three months after we had started dating, my prayers led me to a place of complete peace. Gone were the questions about my readiness to marry again. God had settled my concerns about parenting two more kids as well.

I knew that I loved Lisa. I also knew she loved God, which was at the pinnacle of my desires. A close second was a willingness to love my children and treat them as her own—something she had already demonstrated in our time together. So, I went back to my closest advisers and friends and checked my feelings against their objective opinions. I talked about where my heart and my spirit were leading me, well aware that I had counseled many people in my ministry who let their hearts talk them into things that their heads advised against. I was surprised to find that in my closest circle of friends, not one person had a hesitation about the two of us getting married.

June rolled around. The temperatures in Middle Tennessee were not yet unbearably hot, and the summer days were providing their usual relief from school for the kids. The tenth of June was another of those beautiful summer days. We finished up church that morning, packed the last of our equipment into our trailers at the school where we met for worship, and enjoyed lunch together—Lisa and her girls along with Harrison, Abby, and me. Afterwards, we dropped the kids off at my house and I asked Lisa to go for another ride on the Trace with me in her convertible. Looking back now, I see that it was a bad idea. She froze for a second and immediately offered an excuse for not going. Her first thought was that it was time for another relationship talk—one her heart just wasn't ready for.

She was right about my intent to have a relationship talk, just not the kind she imagined.

After a little encouragement, Lisa relented. We told the kids where we were headed and said good-bye. All four of them were snickering and whispering as we walked out the door, bursting to hold the secret that I had shared with them just the night before. I had entrusted Harrison, Abby, and Lisa's two girls with the news that I'd be popping the question today.

Lisa and I drove up onto the Trace and talked about what the week held for both of us. I looked for a place where we could pull off and stop to talk; meanwhile, Lisa secretly prayed that every parking spot along the way would be full and there'd be no place for a private conversation.

Her prayers must have worked. Once we had driven a few miles without finding any place to park, I decided to shift my plans.

I'm not sure how subtle I was, but I purposely sniffled a couple of times and then asked Lisa, "Do you mind looking in the glove compartment and getting me a napkin? My allergies are driving me crazy."

Lisa was still as nervous as she could be, convinced that the end of our relationship was near. "There aren't any napkins in there," she declared. She was as stiff as a board and staring straight ahead as we zipped through the summer heat.

"Yeah, there are," I replied. "They're in the back of the glove compartment."

"There aren't any there. It's my car; I would know something like that," she countered, refusing to pop open the compartment.

"I promise you, there are some in there. I put them there this week. Just look for me, please."

She reluctantly leaned forward and pushed the button, dropping the door open. She must have been thinking to herself, *Why in the world are you so focused on those stupid napkins when our relationship is at stake?*

Sure enough, there were no napkins—a fact she quickly pointed out to me.

"I told you, they are in the back there. Right behind that box."

Lisa quickly shoved the box aside, still not comprehending that the napkins were not the point of this little exercise. She shuffled the items in the compartment back and forth, trying to prove to me that they weren't there so I would give up. Suddenly, on the third or fourth sweep of her hand, she noticed the box. It was gray . . . a ring box. She pulled it out, her mouth wide open and her eyes as bright as the afternoon sun. She turned to face me, half in shock, half unsure that the box held what she thought it did.

She began to cry great big tears. She cried and laughed, cried and laughed, all the while clutching the box as we wound our way down the road.

Finally I chided, "You know, I've got a question to ask you, but I really need for you to open the box."

With one quick motion she flipped the top—and the tears just flooded her eyes. Each tear rolled down her cheek and into the corners of her very wide grin.

"Rid." I love it when she calls me that. I especially did at that moment. "What in the world . . . ?" Her question trailed off into another loud laugh.

"So, Lisa, I was wondering . . . would you be willing to marry me?" I glanced from the road to Lisa and back again as we continued to move along the Trace.

She answered yes, but she really didn't have to. Her ear-to-ear grin was a sure giveaway.

God was indeed up to something.

As we left the Trace and headed back toward Franklin, Lisa asked me, "Where are we going now?" recognizing that we weren't en route to my house.

I eased her car into the neighborhood where her parents lived.

"Where are we going?" she asked again.

"I've got to go see your parents now. I know we're a little older, but I'd like to ask your parents' permission to marry you. They have been through a long journey with you and your girls. I want to make sure they are okay with my kids and me being a part of that."

Lisa shook her head and said thank you as we pulled into their driveway.

The next few weeks were literally a blur. We got engaged on June tenth. Our goal was to be married on July fifteenth— my fortieth birthday and just five months and six days after our first meeting. In all my years of ministry, I had warned couples in our position to be cautious about jumping back into marriage and to think carefully about the ins and outs of what blending a family might look like. Yet here I was, pulling off a wedding in less than forty days from start to finish.

Of course, the responses to our announcement ran the gamut. There were those who gave their unfettered support to both of us. Many of them had walked with us through our personal journeys and were thrilled to see what God was doing for us and in us.

There were others who gave their conditional support, skeptical that it would work or that it would get very far, but happy if it did.

Then there were plenty who were adamantly opposed to the very idea of a minister dating or marrying a woman with two failed marriages. Their opposition took many forms. Some were upfront and vocal about their stance, quoting many of the same verses from the Bible that I had studied during my own soul-searching. Others took portions of Scripture and twisted them to fit their arguments. There were still others who said little to our faces; they simply walked away. They walked away from our church; some even walked away from our friendship. This was difficult to watch and, of course, more difficult to experience. But hindsight was showing me that this was just one of the many reasons God had taken me through my own period of self-examination: He wanted me to be sure for myself so that I could withstand the second-guessing of others.

One particular friend comes to mind. Like many others who opposed Lisa's and my relationship, I wasn't sure what served as the underlying reason for this woman's opposition. I just knew that it was real and unyielding. So much so that she and her family pulled out of our church and chose to go elsewhere.

My heart broke when people came to that decision. I was sure that God was ready for me to make this move. Why couldn't they just be happy for me?

Many months later, this woman phoned me one day at the church office. Not sure of what to expect after all that time, I answered the call. We chatted briefly and caught up as if nothing had happened, then she turned to the reason for her call.

"Ridley, I want to apologize. When you and Lisa made your announcement, I should have trusted you. I should have believed that you had prayed through this decision and that you were sure about what you were doing. I wish I had given Lisa a chance and gotten to know her. I'm happy you guys are doing great and thankful that the church and your marriage are doing well."

It took a lot for my friend to respond that way. I am thankful for the character it took to make that phone call. More than that, I'm thankful that when God spoke to her, she listened.

In the weeks just before the wedding, we began the task of blending a family. There were the logistical conversations of where we would live and how we would combine our finances. There were practical things like which kid would use which room in our house and who would share bathrooms. Both Lisa and I felt like we were having all the tough conversations and dealing with the difficult decisions head on. Even so, we were often blindsided by some of the weird and silly things that surfaced. These provided valuable lessons as we talked about our future together and how God could potentially use our journey to help others in theirs.

Then, the week before our wedding, Lisa and I had our first major disagreement. In five months' time we had seldom disagreed on anything—and never enough to really get upset with each other.

It all changed that night.

I don't recall what the argument was about or how long it went on. I do remember thinking how intense and mean it was for both of us. I also remember that much of Lisa's emotion that night centered on the marriage she had left almost four years earlier. It was the first time I had seen those hurt feelings rise to the surface in her. It was also the first time the two of us would use the word *trigger* in reference to what had gone on in her past.

Honestly, it scared me. I was not naïve; I knew there were tremendous amounts of baggage after what Lisa had endured. But it was the first time that I had felt the point of that dagger.

I went to bed that night with a heavy heart over our first argument, even though we had resolved it quickly. I also carried a burden for our future. I knew that if God had seen fit to put our lives together, He had some purpose for it. Marriages don't exist just for our pleasure; they exist so that God can receive glory.

As I drifted off to sleep that night, God comforted me with the reminder that He would never carry me to a place where He would not give me the strength to go.

20

The morning of July 15, 2007, was another brilliant, sunny day in Franklin. It was also a Sunday. But not just any Sunday. Lisa and I were getting married.

Anybody riding by our house that day would never have suspected the flurry of activity that was going on inside. We had intentionally kept things small and simple. Both of us believed that when you do this the second—or third—time around, it's really about the marriage and less about the wedding. That's probably a worthwhile lesson for most couples. Nevertheless, it was an especially busy morning, and I was a little nervous as I got ready for church.

The source of my jitters was not so much about the wedding that afternoon as it was about the timing of the day. I would, just as on any other Sunday, be at the church by 7:45 a.m. to help our set-up team unload trailers. That would take about an hour. Then I'd rush home to wake the kids and have breakfast with my family, who had gathered in town to help us celebrate the big day.

Following the kitchen cleanup, I would take a quick shower before all of us headed over to the church for our time of worship. Our service would last till about 11:45. I'd need another thirty minutes to help with teardown, while Harrison and Abby would go home with my sister and mom to get ready for the wedding. Then Abby's hair had to be done and Harrison had to get into his tuxedo. The four kids were to serve as our entire wedding party.

After finishing up at the church, I would race home, clean up again, and get dressed in my own tux for the wedding, which was to begin at 1 p.m.

From our house to Lisa's home church was about a twenty-minute drive. The kids and I arrived just before the ceremony was to begin. My sisters took care of getting Abby to the area where Lisa and the other girls were dressing. Harrison followed me around to the back hallway to meet with the pastor who would be officiating the ceremony.

Judging by his actions, I think Harrison may have been just as nervous as I was. He simply could not sit still and chattered incessantly. But my nerves were quickly settling as we got closer to the big moment. The presence of our friends and family was a visual reminder of how much Lisa and I were loved and supported.

I talked with the officiating pastor for just a few minutes and then led Harrison around to the room where Lisa and the girls were. She and I had talked about this ahead of time: Neither of us is superstitious. It was more important to both of us that we have some time together before the ceremony.

Lisa's friend Kate wanted to stop me at the door. I assured her that I had the clearance to see Lisa. Reluctantly, she stepped out of the doorway and let me pass.

In the outer part of the dressing room were Lisa's and my three girls, gorgeously attired for the big event. They were continuing to primp a little, revealing how nervous they were as well. I hugged them and told them how beautiful they looked.

Then the door to the inner room opened behind me and I turned to face Lisa. She looked incredible. Absolutely gorgeous. Whatever bit of nerves had been lingering melted away with that first glance. I stepped into the room, just a little afraid to touch her, thinking I might mess up her dress or her hair. She reached her hand out to mine. She was very relieved that we had made it safely and on time.

"You look incredible, baby," I told her. Looking closer, I could see tears forming in her eyes as a bashful grin broke across her face.

"You look very handsome yourself. I'm glad you're here."

"No other place I'd rather be," I said as I inched closer to her, careful not to step on her shoes.

"Are you sure?" There they were again—the doubts and fears of a broken past and broken promises. Now, I was trying to decide if the tears were tears of joy . . . or fear . . . or a little of both.

"I'm sure. I've told you that before," I gently reminded her. "I'll tell you that for the rest of your life."

This time I could tell the smile was a happy one. Her next question came slowly. " . . . Even if you have to put up with all the baggage and the triggers?"

"Baby, I've got baggage of my own. Who doesn't? I just know that I believe with all my heart that God has put us together in this moment for the rest of our lives. I'm not a quitter or a leaver."

"I love you," she said even more confidently.

"I love you too, Lisa. Are you ready to do this?"

She grinned again, this time bigger than all the rest, and her face flushed with expectation. Her smile could have lit up the darkest moment for me. Her blue eyes gleamed with the hope that comes from knowing that the future is in the hands of One who handles it best.

I turned to close the door to give us a few moments of privacy before the ceremony began. Lisa came closer, leaning her head on my chest, tears in her eyes—just like a February night five months earlier. Holding her tightly, I thanked God for that moment . . . for this woman.

Quietly, in our last few minutes together before the wedding, we began our life together in the best way—the only way—we felt was right: "Jesus, thank You for where we are. Thank You for where You are taking us . . ."

THE NEXT CHAPTER

Who can write a better story than God? It's a question I have asked myself many times as I wait with both an anxious heart and childlike excitement to see what the next pages of His story will hold for all of us. It is a reality I live every single day.

Since getting married, Lisa and I have focused on raising our kids and swirling our family. *Swirling* is a word we chose because we liked it better than *blending*. For those of you who have ever attempted this feat, you know it's a mixed bag of challenges and rewards, emotional highs and intense turmoil. I wouldn't trade it for anything. I was blessed with two beautiful new daughters the day that I married Lisa. They have brought me many smiles—and a few gray hairs too, just as Abby and Harrison have.

Of course, Abby and Harrison continue to delight my heart as well. They were six and nine, respectively, at the time of the accident. Since then, both have continued to grow in wisdom and maturity—which is all any parent can ask for. They have loved me in ways that a daddy deeply desires but seldom feels he deserves. As the years pass, I see

Sarah Ellen's predictions coming true—Harrison is very much the image of me in personality and appearance. The same can be said of Abby in regards to her mother. She looks more and more like Sarah Ellen with every year that passes. I thank God daily that He saw fit that April day to spare these children who inspire me to be better. But I am doubly blessed in that God also added three beautiful ladies to fill our house with laughter.

In February 2011, my life took an unexpected twist again. I had been in church ministry since age nineteen. From 2004 to 2011, I served as pastor of Ridgeview Community Church in Franklin, Tennessee—the church my family and I started when we moved back to the area. On the side, I had continued to take advantage of each opportunity that was given to me to share Josh's story. I knew that every time the story was told, it was another chance for someone to be inspired and to hear about faith, hope, healing, and forgiveness.

By February 2011, the invitations to speak had grown more numerous. I finally informed Lisa one day that a decision loomed ahead for us, because to continue at the pace we were going would mean both the church and Ridley Barron Ministries (RBM) would suffer. Believing I would have to step down from one or the other, we began to pray intensely about what God might want and what that would look like. There was security in my church: people I loved, a job I was comfortable with, and a steady paycheck. My plan had been to invest my life in Ridgeview and watch it "grow up."

God's plan was otherwise. He made it very clear to Lisa and me through a series of events that RBM was where He wanted us full time. So I stepped down from the pastorate in May 2011, giving a very tearful resignation to the people I loved most. Their support had been instrumental in moving me toward healing, and their love had carried me during the darkest hours of those post-accident days.

As the appointments calendar emptied and the phone grew quiet that summer, I wasn't exactly sure what it meant other than I was sitting at home doing a lot of chores that I had fallen behind on. Frankly, I got scared. Had I misread God? Misunderstood what He was trying to say to Lisa and me? I shared those thoughts with my board during a prayer retreat. Those men and their wives spoke truth and wisdom into my life that weekend. Their prayers and support energized me to keep moving forward—to keep doing the next right thing in anticipation of God's next move. I walked away from that weekend more convinced than ever that God still wanted me pastoring—but not in a church. No, His direction for me was to minister to those outside the walls of the traditional church and bring the hope and healing we talk about through Josh's story.

I was down to the last event on my schedule—speaking to a hospital system in Texas—when the first phone call in this new venture came through. Then another and another. God was showing that He would provide, that He would open the door to share my story wherever He chose.

Today, He is still very much at work, and Lisa and I are doing our best to keep up with Him. But with each new opportunity comes this incredible feeling that Sarah and Josh's lives are counting for something far bigger than we could have ever dreamed. Healthcare workers are being challenged. Families are being mended. Relationships have been restored. In far distant corners of this country where I might never have been allowed to go otherwise, I am being given the tremendous privilege of standing in front of people just like me who need hope, healing, and forgiveness. For that reason, as long as God wills it, I will keep telling Josh's story—our story. It is, after all, written by the very best Author I know.

A FINAL WORD

Over the past several years I have been blessed with the opportunity to crisscross this country and share the events that touched our family. In those instances, I've had the pleasure of getting to know some exceptional people and hear their stories. It's been an answer to prayer to see how the circumstances from our family's tragedy have served to encourage and lift up other people.

Typically, during the question-and-answer time that I offer, I'll get asked about a half dozen questions that take the story a little deeper. Afterwards, Lisa and I make ourselves available because we know that the story of the accident and its aftermath can bring up some tough memories for people in the audience. We truly want to bless those who God brings onto our path.

A common question that gets asked as part of those conversations centers on the issue of forgiveness. People want to know how or why I chose to forgive the driver of the vehicle and the pharmacist who gave Josh his overdose. I can honestly say this is a question I have pondered many times myself. But the first step involved an important decision.

On Saturday, April 10, 2004, I laid in that hospital bed waiting for the hospital staff to bring Harrison and Abby into the room. I knew that I was going to have to break the news to them about their mom's death and Josh's condition. But there was something looming even larger for me—a thought I had begun to ponder almost the instant Harrison's voice woke me in that van the day before.

Yes, I was full of questions: What about the future? Could I be the dad my kids needed me to be? Could I continue to live life and really enjoy it? Would depression consume me or fears paralyze me? But when the door opened and Harrison was wheeled into my room, the questions in my head were disrupted by a very "loud" thought: *He needs you! So do Abby and Josh. And for their lives to be anything near what God desires them to be, you must choose to forgive.*

The true meaning of forgiveness often eludes us until we are forced into a place where the choice to forgive or hold a grudge has to be made. But the misconceptions that come with some of the questions I get about how to forgive are numerous.

First of all, I am usually asked something like, "How did you find the ability to forgive the driver that hit your family and the people involved in Josh's death?" This question implies that forgiveness is some innate trait that we simply have to dig up and put into practice. I don't think the ability to forgive is something we're given at birth as much as it is a concept we learn. In fact, I believe we are born with quite the opposite desire: revenge. In the years since that fateful April day, I have felt that desire surge within me more times than I can remember. Rather than choosing to forgive, everything inside of me wanted to make someone pay for what had happened. I didn't want to offer forgiveness; I wanted to offer pain that matched my own. But in my more sensible moments, I would see that there was nothing to be gained from revenge. Hatred and anger would not bring Josh back, nor give me the privilege of holding Sarah again.

I also hear questions that imply that forgiveness is something you do and it is over with. A young lady stopped me after a conference in the Midwest one night. She sounded like so many others I had met . . . With tears in her eyes, she told me her story of loss. Then she asked, "Mr. Barron, you have made forgiveness sound so easy. Now that you have forgiven these people, how do you move on?"

I'll share with you what I shared with her that night: forgiveness is not some one-time event; it is a daily decision that we have to make.

Every single day for the rest of my life, I am given the option to relive the past; I am given the option of holding onto bitterness over past events. Am I tempted by the opportunity to hold a grudge or be bitter? You bet. I think I would be something less than human if the loss of my wife and son didn't cause such feelings. However, I believe that it's far more important that I live life in light of what my future holds rather than in light of what my past has done to me.

Well-meaning individuals along the way would try to encourage me to channel my anger toward something "constructive." I don't think that's a reality. Bitterness is a poison that kills no one but the person who holds it. As I have heard other pastors share, it is like drinking a poisonous drink and waiting for your enemy to die. For me, to hold on would have done nothing but eat me alive like a cancer, making me an out-of-touch dad and a shell of the man I should be.

I think the key to forgiveness in any situation comes to the importance of perspective. If I believe that this life is all I have, then I fight tooth-and-nail to preserve it, to milk every possibility from every second I am given. If I believe that all I am given is the seventy-plus years of the average man, then my mortality scares me and the failure of others rattles my being and shakes my security.

On the other hand, my personal beliefs regarding the future and what it holds keep me from clinging too tightly to the present, and even less so to the past. The choice I have made to forgive has enabled me to live a life of freedom I would not have known otherwise. Bitterness cages us and limits our ability to embrace life.

The question of how *do* you forgive can only be answered by saying, "One day at a time." Some days, it is truly one *moment* at a time.

The question of how *can* I forgive is an even deeper one. The answer for me is as sure as the words that fill these pages. It goes back to the very foundational instructions of my parents and the encouraging words of other significant people in my life. Mostly, it goes back to Jesus Christ.

Here is where some of you will tune me out. You will choose, because of your own personal beliefs, to skip the last few words of this book. It is your choice. It always has been. But for those of you who choose to read further, I will tell you that forgiveness—in its purest, simplest meaning—could only be accomplished for me by understanding what Jesus did 2,000 years ago. I did not deserve the forgiveness Jesus offered. He gave it anyway. He did not give because of my efforts or my achievements. In fact, everything about me screams for justice and punishment.

No, Jesus forgave because He was compelled to out of love for me. In the nights of that unforgettable spring in South Georgia, I was confronted consistently by the reality that because I was forgiven, I could do no less for those who had wronged me. Let me say it again: it has not nor will it ever be an easy choice. But for me, it is the only right one if I am to see God bring good from the tragedy of April 9, 2004.

If these words have encouraged you, I would love to hear about it. Visit our website—www.ridleybarron.com—or our Facebook page at Ridley Barron Ministries.

I am inspired by the stories of others who have been

touched by Josh and Sarah's story. My hope is that the deaths of my family members may lead others to find the life—the full and joyful life—that is available through the receiving and granting of forgiveness.

May God bless you as you make *your* choice.

~Ridley

ACKNOWLEDGMENTS

I'd like to acknowledge the following people who encouraged, supported, challenged, and prayed for me from day to day until this project was done:

Kris Bearss, who headed up this project, and her team of publishing experts. I told you many times throughout this process that you made writing a book more fun than I thought possible. I hope it's worth every bit of energy you put into it.

The Christ followers of GracePointe Church in Douglas, Georgia; Forest Hills Baptist Church in Nashville, Tennessee; and Ridgeview Community Church in Franklin, Tennessee. You were the model of a loving family in the months after the wreck. I will forever remember every act of love you showed us during those days. It was your prayers and support that helped me as my kids and I began our new life.

Gran and Pops—Jim and Sharon DeHart—and Lisa's brother, Thad. Thanks for welcoming me and my two kids into your family. You are a "bonus" blessing in the life I've been given.

Tricia and Neil Stevens and Clay and Amy Trimble. Thank you for being my family both then and now. I love you guys dearly and am grateful to God that He gave me you.

My dad, Ridley Jr., my mother, Nadine, my sisters Harriet and Tonda, and their husbands, Richard and Keith. Long before the tragedy in 2004, it was you who taught me lessons about the kind of man I would need to be as I grew older, and you who kicked me in the seat of the pants when I needed it. Who knew the lessons of childhood and youth would play such a critical role in helping me heal and move on?

My family. Most men count themselves blessed to have been loved once in this life. I find I am blessed by the love of an amazing woman, Lisa, and four incredible kids who make my heart swell with pride: Morgan, Harrison, Abby, and Landon. I am thankful for each of you and the encouragement you have given me in this project. I pray every day that I am becoming more of the husband and father that you need and that God desires.

From the ashes of **Ridley Barron**'s story has arisen a ministry in which he and his wife, Lisa, work to encourage others in the medical industry and in faith-based settings. Ridley has emerged as a nationally known speaker on topics such as quality of care, survivor guilt, sentinel events, and the second victim in hospital errors. He also leads marriage and family retreats, young adult and youth conferences, and leadership training for many organizations. Lisa's own reputation has grown as she speaks to encourage women around the country with words gained from practical insight, laughter, and personal faith. Today, Ridley and Lisa live in the Nashville, Tennessee, area with their four kids.

For information or scheduling for
Ridley Barron Ministries, contact:

Kimberly Johnson,
Public Relations Director
kimberly@ridleybarron.com
615-392-0772
info@ridleybarron.com

Or find us at:
www.ridleybarron.com
facebook.com/RidleyBarronMinistries